Lecture Notes in Computer Science   14202

Founding Editors

Gerhard Goos
Juris Hartmanis

The series Lecture Notes in Computer Science (LNCS), including its subseries Lecture Notes in Artificial Intelligence (LNAI) and Lecture Notes in Bioinformatics (LNBI), has established itself as a medium for the publication of new developments in computer science and information technology research, teaching, and education.

LNCS enjoys close cooperation with the computer science R & D community, the series counts many renowned academics among its volume editors and paper authors, and collaborates with prestigious societies. Its mission is to serve this international community by providing an invaluable service, mainly focused on the publication of conference and workshop proceedings and postproceedings. LNCS commenced publication in 1973.

Yujiu Yang · Xiaohui Wang · Liang-Jie Zhang
Editors

Artificial Intelligence and Mobile Services – AIMS 2023

12th International Conference
Held as Part of the Services Conference Federation, SCF 2023
Honolulu, HI, USA, September 23–26, 2023
Proceedings

Springer

Editors
Yujiu Yang 🆔
Tsinghua University
Shenzhen, China

Xiaohui Wang 🆔
University of Science and Technology
Beijing, China

Liang-Jie Zhang 🆔
Shenzhen Entrepreneurship and Innovation
Federation
Shenzhen, China

ISSN 0302-9743   ISSN 1611-3349 (electronic)
Lecture Notes in Computer Science
ISBN 978-3-031-45139-3   ISBN 978-3-031-45140-9 (eBook)
https://doi.org/10.1007/978-3-031-45140-9

This Springer imprint is published by the registered company Springer Nature Switzerland AG
The registered company address is: Gewerbestrasse 11, 6330 Cham, Switzerland

Paper in this product is recyclable.

Preface

The 2023 International Conference on AI & Mobile Services (AIMS 2023) aimed to provide an international forum dedicated to exploring different aspects of AI (from technologies to approaches and algorithms) and mobile services (from business management to computing systems, algorithms, and applications) and to promoting technological innovations in research and development of mobile services, including, but not limited to, wireless & sensor networks, mobile & wearable computing, mobile enterprise & eCommerce, ubiquitous collaborative & social services, machine-to-machine & Internet-of-things clouds, cyber-physical integration, and big data analytics for mobility-enabled services.

AIMS 2023 was a member of the Services Conference Federation (SCF). SCF 2023 had the following 10 collocated service-oriented sister conferences: 2023 International Conference on Web Services (ICWS 2023), 2023 International Conference on Cloud Computing (CLOUD 2023), 2023 International Conference on Services Computing (SCC 2023), 2023 International Conference on Big Data (BigData 2023), 2023 International Conference on AI & Mobile Services (AIMS 2023), 2023 World Congress on Services (SERVICES 2023), 2023 International Conference on Internet of Things (ICIOT 2023), 2023 International Conference on Cognitive Computing (ICCC 2023), 2023 International Conference on Edge Computing (EDGE 2023), and 2023 International Conference on Blockchain (ICBC 2023).

This volume presents the accepted papers for AIMS 2023. AIMS 2023's major topics included but were not limited to: AI Modeling, AI Analysis, AI & Mobile Applications, AI Architecture, AI Management, AI Engineering, Mobile backend as a service (MBaaS), and User experience of AI & mobile services.

We accepted 9 full papers. Each was reviewed and selected by two or three independent members of the AIMS 2023 International Program Committee. We are pleased to thank the authors whose submissions and participation made this conference possible. We also want to express our thanks to the Program Committee members, for their dedication in helping to organize the conference and reviewing the submissions. We appreciate your great contributions as volunteers, authors, and conference participants in the fast-growing worldwide services innovations community.

September 2023

Yujiu Yang
Xiaohui Wang
Liang-Jie Zhang

Organization

General Chairs

Ruifeng Xu   Harbin Institute of Technology, China
Xiuqin Pan   Minzu University of China, China

Program Chairs

Yujiu Yang   Tsinghua University, China
Xiaohui Wang   University of Science and Technology Beijing, China

Services Conference Federation (SCF 2023)

General Chairs

Ali Arsanjani   Google, USA
Wu Chou   Essenlix Corporation, USA

Coordinating Program Chair

Liang-Jie Zhang   Kingdee International Software Group Co., Ltd., China

CFO and International Affairs Chair

Min Luo   Georgia Tech, USA

Operations Committee

Jing Zeng   China Gridcom Co., Ltd., China
Yishuang Ning   Tsinghua University, China
Sheng He   Tsinghua University, China

Steering Committee

Calton Pu (Co-chair)	Georgia Tech, USA
Liang-Jie Zhang (Co-chair)	Shenzhen Entrepreneurship and Innovation Federation, China

AIMS 2022 Program Committee

Na Sun	Minzu University of China, China
Hong Zhang	Minzu University of China, China
Zhongjian Dai	Beijing Institute of Technology, China
Guangming Li	Dongguan University of Technology, China
XiaoKun Wang	University of Science and Technology Beijing, China
XiuQin Pan	Minzu University of China, China
XiaoYuan Li	Zhengzhou University, China

Conference Sponsor – Services Society

The Services Society (S2) is a non-profit professional organization that has been created to promote worldwide research and technical collaboration in services innovations among academia and industrial professionals. Its members are volunteers from industry and academia with common interests. S2 is registered in the USA as a "501(c) organization", which means that it is an American tax-exempt nonprofit organization. S2 collaborates with other professional organizations to sponsor or co-sponsor conferences and to promote an effective services curriculum in colleges and universities. S2 initiates and promotes a "Services University" program worldwide to bridge the gap between industrial needs and university instruction.

The Services Sector has account for 79.5% of the GDP of United States in 2016. The Services Society has formed 10 Special Interest Groups (SIGs) to support technology and domain specific professional activities.

- Special Interest Group on Services Computing (SIG-SC)
- Special Interest Group on Big Data (SIG-BD)
- Special Interest Group on Cloud Computing (SIG-CLOUD)
- Special Interest Group on Artificial Intelligence (SIG-AI)
- Special Interest Group on Metaverse (SIG-Metaverse)

About Services Conference Federation (SCF)

As the founding member of the Services Conference Federation (SCF), the first International Conference on Web Services (ICWS) was held in June 2003 in Las Vegas, USA. Meanwhile, the First International Conference on Web Services - Europe 2003 (ICWS-Europe 2003) was held in Germany in October 2003. ICWS-Europe 2003 was an extended event of the 2003 International Conference on Web Services (ICWS 2003) in Europe. In 2004, ICWS-Europe was changed to the European Conference on Web Services (ECOWS), which was held in Erfurt, Germany. SCF 2019 was held successfully on June 25–30, 2019 in San Diego, USA. Affected by COVID-19, SCF 2020 was successfully held on September 18–20, 2020 over the Internet. SCF 2021 was held virtually over the Internet on December 10–14, 2021. SCF 2022 was successfully held on December 10–14, 2022, Hawaii, USA. To celebrate its 21st birthday, SCF 2023 was held in Honolulu, Hawaii, USA.

In the past 20 years, the ICWS community has been expanded from Web engineering innovations to scientific research for the whole services industry. The service delivery platforms have been expanded to mobile platforms, Internet of Things, cloud computing, and edge computing. The services ecosystem has gradually been enabled, value added, and intelligence embedded through enabling technologies such as big data, artificial intelligence, and cognitive computing. In the coming years, all transactions with multiple parties involved will be transformed to blockchain.

Based on technology trends and best practices in the field, SCF will continue serving as the conference umbrella's code name for all services-related conferences. SCF 2023 defined the future of New ABCDE (AI, Blockchain, Cloud, BigData & IOT) as we enter the 5G for Services Era. The theme of SCF 2023 was Digital Transformation. SCF 2023's 10 co-located theme topic conferences all centered around "services", while each focused on exploring different themes (web-based services, cloud-based services, Big Data-based services, services innovation lifecycle, AI-driven ubiquitous services, blockchain-driven trust service-ecosystems, industry-specific services and applications, and emerging service-oriented technologies). SCF includes 10 service-oriented conferences: ICWS, CLOUD, SCC, BigData Congress, AIMS, SERVICES, ICIOT, EDGE, ICCC, and ICBC. The SCF 2023 members are listed as follows:

[1] The 2023 International Conference on Web Services (ICWS 2023, http://icws. org/) was the flagship theme-topic conference for Web-based services, featuring Web services modeling, development, publishing, discovery, composition, testing, adaptation, and delivery, as well as the latest API standards.
[2] The 2023 International Conference on Cloud Computing (CLOUD 2023, http:// thecloudcomputing.org/) was the flagship theme-topic conference for modeling, developing, publishing, monitoring, managing, and delivering XaaS (everything as a service) in the context of various types of cloud environments.

[3] The 2023 International Conference on Big Data (BigData 2023, http://bigdat acongress.org/) was the emerging theme-topic conference for the scientific and engineering innovations of big data.

[4] The 2023 International Conference on Services Computing (SCC 2023, http://the scc.org/) was the flagship theme-topic conference for services innovation lifecycle that includes enterprise modeling, business consulting, solution creation, services orchestration, services optimization, services management, services marketing, and business process integration and management.

[5] The 2023 International Conference on AI & Mobile Services (AIMS 2023, http:// ai1000.org/) was the emerging theme-topic conference for the science and technology of artificial intelligence, and the development, publication, discovery, orchestration, invocation, testing, delivery, and certification of AI-enabled services and mobile applications.

[6] The 2023 International Conference on Metaverse (METAVERSE 2023, http://met averse1000.org/) put its focus on emerging Metaverse technologies and solutions.

[7] The 2023 International Conference on Cognitive Computing (ICCC 2023, http://the cognitivecomputing.org/) put its focus on the Sensing Intelligence (SI) as a Service (SIaaS) that makes systems listen, speak, see, smell, taste, understand, interact, and walk in the context of scientific research and engineering solutions.

[8] The 2023 International Conference on Internet of Things (ICIOT 2023, http:// iciot.org/) put its focus on the creation of Internet of Things technologies and development of IOT services.

[9] The 2023 International Conference on Edge Computing (EDGE 2023, http://theedg ecomputing.org/) put its focus on the state of the art and practice of edge computing including but not limited to localized resource sharing, connections with the cloud, and 5G devices and applications.

[10] The 2023 International Conference on Blockchain (ICBC 2023, http://blockchai n1000.org/) concentrated on blockchain-based services and enabling technologies.

Some highlights of SCF 2023 are shown below:

- **Bigger Platform:** The 10 collocated conferences (SCF 2023) received sponsorship from the Services Society, which is the world-leading not-for-profit organization (501 c(3)) dedicated to the service of more than 30,000 worldwide Services Computing researchers and practitioners. A bigger platform means bigger opportunities for all volunteers, authors, and participants. Meanwhile, Springer provided sponsorship to best paper awards and other professional activities. All the 10 conference proceedings of SCF 2023 were published by Springer and indexed in ISI Conference Proceedings Citation Index (included in Web of Science), Engineering Index EI (Compendex and Inspec databases), DBLP, Google Scholar, IO-Port, MathSciNet, Scopus, and ZBlMath.
- **Brighter Future:** While celebrating the 2023 version of ICWS, SCF 2023 highlighted the Fourth International Conference on Blockchain (ICBC 2023) to build the fundamental infrastructure for enabling secure and trusted services ecosystems. It will also lead our community members to create their own brighter future.
- **Better Model:** SCF 2023 continued to leverage the invented Conference Blockchain Model (CBM) to innovate the organizing practices for all the 10 theme conferences.

Contents

Contents

Research Track

Artificial Bee Colony Algorithm Based on Improved Search Strategy

Sumin Li[1], Weiyao Zhang[1], Jiatao Hao[1], Ruixiang Li[1(✉)], and Juan Chen[2]

[1] School of Information Engineering, Minzu University of China, Beijing 10081, China
{smli,22302039,21011640}@muc.edu.cn, ruixiang0822@163.com

[2] China National Software and Service Company Limited, Beijing 10081, China

Abstract. The standard Artificial Bee Colony (ABC) algorithm exhibits slow convergence speed and a tendency to get trapped in local optima under certain circumstances. To overcome these limitations, researchers have proposed a new ABC algorithm (GABC) by using a modified search strategy. During the process of searching for solutions, the GABC algorithm incorporates some randomly selected individuals and the global best individual. However, the GABC algorithm still has drawbacks such as low search accuracy and slow convergence speed. In response to these issues, an improved artificial bee colony algorithm (IABC) is proposed in this paper. The IABC algorithm introduces a dynamic inertia weight factor based on the GABC algorithm. A set of standard test functions are used to test the optimization of the improved artificial bee colony algorithm. Experimental results demonstrate that the proposed algorithm outperforms both the standard ABC algorithm and the GABC algorithm in terms of search accuracy and convergence speed.

Keywords: Artificial bee colony · the global best individual · dynamic inertia weight factor

1 Introduction

The Artificial Bee Colony (ABC) algorithm was introduced by Karaboga in 2005 as a novel optimization algorithm based on the foraging behavior of honeybees. Its purpose was to solve multi-variable function optimization problems [1]. In 2014, Zhang proposed an improved version of the standard ABC algorithm to address its shortcomings such as slow convergence speed and premature convergence. The improved algorithm utilizes a random dynamic local search operator to perform local search on the current best food source, thereby accelerating the convergence speed. Additionally, a selection probability based on sorting is employed instead of relying solely on fitness to maintain population diversity and avoid premature convergence [2]. In 2015, Pan et al. proposed a new ABC algorithm (GABC) by using a modified search strategy inspired by a particle update model designed for Particle Swarm Optimization (PSO) by Mahmoodabadi et al. in 2014. Experimental results demonstrated that this improvement enhances the exploration capability of the ABC algorithm [3]. In 2018, Jin et al. drew inspiration from the Multi-Elite Artificial Bee Colony Optimization algorithm and introduced elite individuals and the global best individual in the bee colony to enhance the exploration of global optimal solutions [4]. In the same year, Chen et al. applied a tournament selection strategy to replace the original roulette wheel selection method to improve the issue of premature convergence. They also changed the replacement method for unchanged individuals, introducing a proportional replacement of individuals with the same optimal value. This approach preserves the current best solution while also having the ability to escape local optima [5]. In 2021, Su utilized a group collaboration mechanism in the ABC algorithm. During the employee bee phase, a large-step neighborhood search strategy was employed to enhance the exploration capability of the solution space. In the onlooker bee phase, a small-step neighborhood search strategy was used to improve the convergence accuracy of the solutions [6]. Wang et al. proposed an improved ABC algorithm in 2021 by enhancing the generation method of initial solutions and modifying the operations of three types of bees. These modifications aimed to enhance the optimization ability and robustness of the algorithm, as well as address the problem of getting trapped in local optima [7]. In 2022, Zhang et al. addressed the issue of poor stability in the ABC algorithm by introducing a chaotic initialization strategy. They applied a dynamic hybrid search strategy during the employee bee and onlooker bee phases to improve the algorithm's search traversal. Additionally, they incorporated elite solution information during the onlooker bee phase to balance global exploration and local exploitation capabilities [8]. Ren et al. combined the crossover mechanism with the global optimal-guided ABC algorithm to enhance the colony's exploration capability. They introduced the concept of sensitivity in the onlooker bee selection strategy to increase population diversity and avoid local optima [9]. Wang et al. replaced the onlooker bee search scheme with a probability-based reverse learning during the onlooker bee phase of the ABC algorithm. This modification effectively improved the optimization speed and convergence accuracy of the algorithm [10].

To overcome the issues of low search accuracy and slow convergence speed in the GABC, this paper proposes an Improved Artificial Bee Colony algorithm (IABC) based on the modified search strategy introduced in reference [3]. The IABC algorithm incorporates a dynamic inertia weight factor to enhance both global and local search capabilities. Furthermore, new search strategies are employed in the employed bee phase and onlooker bee phase to improve the algorithm's search performance. The proposed algorithm is compared with the standard ABC algorithm and the GABC algorithm using eight standard test functions, and its search performance is validated through experiments.

2   Artificial Bee Colony

The principle of the ABC is inspired by the foraging behavior of honeybees. During foraging, they first send out some bees to explore the surrounding environment and search for new food sources. After a bee finds a food source, it communicates the information to other bees, who then join in collecting the food. Throughout this process, bees continuously update their positions to achieve optimal foraging efficiency.

In the ABC algorithm, the search space is considered as a beehive, with numerous bees representing potential solutions. Each bee's position corresponds to the variable values of a solution. The algorithm consists of three types of bees: employed bees, onlooker bees, and scout bees.

Employed bees: Employed bees are responsible for searching for new solutions around their current positions. Each employed bee randomly selects a new position near its current position and calculates corresponding fitness value. If the fitness value of the new position is better than the current position, the bee updates its position to the new position.

Onlooker bees: Onlooker bees select employed bees to follow based on a roulette wheel selection rule. They then search for new solutions around the chosen employed bee's position and calculate their fitness value. The onlooker bees greedily choose the best solution and replace their own position if it is superior.

Scout bees: If a bee fails to find a better solution within a specified threshold, indicating it may be trapped in a local optimum, it becomes a scout bee. Scout bees randomly fly to new positions and calculate their fitness value to explore alternative solutions.

In the ABC algorithm, the bees' positions represent variable values of potential solutions, and their fitness values represent the quality of those solutions. The goal of the ABC algorithm is to continuously update the bees' positions to search for the global optimal solution.

The basic process of the ABC algorithm is as follows:

Initialization: Randomly generate a set of initial solutions known as the bee population. Each bee represents a solution x_{id}, which can be expressd as:

$$x_{id} = L_d + \text{rand}(0, 1)(U_d - L_d) \tag{1}$$

where x_{id} is the component of the i-th solution in the d-th dimension, $i \in \{1, 2, \ldots, SN\}$, SN is the number of bees, U_d and L_d represent the upper and lower bounds of the d-th dimension in the feasible solution space, respectively. $\text{rand}(0, 1)$ is a random number between 0 and 1.

Employed Bees Phase: Each employed bee explores the neighborhood of its current solution. They search for new solutions within the vicinity of their current solution using Eq. (2) based on the quality evaluation of the current solution.

$$x_{id}^{\text{new}} = x_{id} + \alpha \times \varphi(x_{id} - x_{jd}) \tag{2}$$

where d is the dimension of the current position, x_{id}^{new} is the new solution searched, $j \in \{1, 2, \ldots, SN\}$, $j \neq i$, which means a bee not equal to i is randomly selected among SN bees, φ is a random number uniformly distributed between -1 and 1, which determines the perturbation degree, and α is the acceleration coefficient (typically set to 1).

Onlooker Bees Phase: Bees exchange information among themselves. Then, based on Eq. (3), the onlooker bees calculate the selection probabilities to determine the probability of following each employed bee.

$$p_i = \frac{fit_i}{\sum_{i=1}^{SN} fit_i} \tag{3}$$

The onlooker bees choose employed bees to follow based on the selection probabilities p_i and generate new solutions in the vicinity of the employed bees using Eq. (2). The fitness values of the new solutions are evaluated, and the onlooker bees select the better solution based on a greedy strategy.

Scout Bees Phase: This phase determines if there are any solutions that need to be abandoned. If such solutions exist, a random replacement solution is generated using Eq. (1). This step enhances the global search capability of the algorithm.

Termination Criteria: Steps 2 to 4 are iteratively executed until a termination criterion is met, such as reaching the maximum number of iterations or finding a satisfactory solution.

The artificial bee colony algorithm can be used to solve various optimization problems in different fields, such as signal, image, and video processing, topology optimization, and artificial intelligence. Some of the real-world application scenarios for the artificial bee colony algorithm are:

Image segmentation: The artificial bee colony algorithm can be used to partition an image into meaningful regions based on some criteria, such as color, intensity, or texture.

Feature selection: The artificial bee colony algorithm can be used to select a subset of features from a large set of features that are relevant for a specific task, such as classification or clustering.

Path planning: The artificial bee colony algorithm can be used to find the optimal or near-optimal path for a robot or a vehicle to move from one location to another while avoiding obstacles and minimizing the cost.

3 Improved Artificial Bee Colony

The ABC algorithm is a swarm intelligence algorithm that has many advantages. However, one of its drawbacks is that each bee selects the optimal solution based on Eq. (2), which relies on the quality of the surrounding bees. This can result in slow convergence and susceptibility to local optima. To effectively tackle the aforementioned problems, Pan et al. introduced an enhanced ABC algorithm called GABC. This algorithm incorporates a new search strategy that includes a combination of randomly selected individuals and the global best individual to enhance the algorithm's exploration capability and accelerate convergence speed. The improved search strategy proposed by Pan is as follows:

$$x_{id}^{\text{new}} = \text{gbest}_d + \phi_{id} \cdot \left(2 \cdot \text{gbest}_d - x_{id} - x_{jd}\right) \qquad (4)$$

where d is the dimension of the current position, x_{id}^{new} is the new solution searched, gbest_d is the global optimum. x_{id} is the component of the i solution in the d-th dimension, ϕ_{id} is a random number uniformly distributed between -1 and 1.

The difference between Eq. (4) and Eq. (2) lies in using the weighted average of three positions to update the velocity, instead of only considering the current position and a random position. This modification may lead to faster convergence of the algorithm by increasing the diversity in the search space. However, it may also result in unstable convergence performance since using three positions to update the velocity can cause the bees to jump too far in the search space, making it difficult to converge stably to the optimal solution. The algorithm should focus on the bees' global search capability in the early stages of the search and shift towards their local search capability in the later stages. Therefore, the parameters of the particle swarm algorithm should not remain fixed, and the inertia weight factor should vary with the number of iterations.

It can be observed that the mentioned equation does not incorporate any dynamic adjustment of the inertia weight factor. To further improve the development efficiency and search capability of the algorithm, and to prevent it from getting trapped in local optima, this paper proposes an improved Artificial Bee Colony algorithm (IABC). This algorithm introduces a dynamic inertia weight factor into the search strategy of GABC, where the value of the inertia weight factor can affect the global and local search capabilities of the algorithm. Shi proposed a linearly decreasing inertia weight particle swarm algorithm in reference [11], where the inertia weight gradually decreases as the number of iterations increases. The paper linearly decreases the inertia weight from 0.9 to 0.4, resulting in significant improvement in algorithm performance. This approach allows the particle swarm algorithm to have better global search capability in the early stages and better local search capability in the later stages. The inertia weight is adjusted according to the following equation.

$$\omega = \omega_{max} - \frac{\omega_{max} - \omega_{min}}{T} \times t \tag{5}$$

where ω_{max}, ω_{min} is the maximum and minimum values within a range, respectively, T is the maximum number of iterations, and t is the current number of iterations.

Inspired by the literature [3] and literature [11], a new search strategy is designed in this paper as follows.

Building upon the insights from references [3] and [11], this paper proposes a novel search strategy as follows.

During the employed bee phase, the search strategy is enhanced as follows:

$$x_{id}^{new} = \text{gbest}_d + \omega \cdot \phi_{id} \cdot \left(2 \cdot \text{gbest}_d - x_{id} - x_{jd}\right) \tag{6}$$

During the onlooker bee phase, the search strategy is improved as follows:

$$x_{id}^{new} = \omega \cdot \text{gbest}_d + \phi_{id} \cdot \left(2 \cdot \text{gbest}_d - x_{id} - x_{jd}\right) \tag{7}$$

In the initial stages of the algorithm, a larger value of ω is used, and it is dynamically adjusted linearly during the iteration process to gradually decrease its value. This ensures that the bees explore the solution space quickly with larger steps in the early iterations. In the later stages of the algorithm, a smaller value of ω is used to converge more precisely to the global optimum. This approach balances the convergence speed and accuracy while increasing the algorithm's robustness and flexibility.

The implementation steps for the improved algorithm are as follows:

Step 1: Initialize the population of solutions based on Eq. (1).
Step 2: Calculate the fitness value for each bee in the population.
Step 3: Repeat the following steps until the termination condition is met:
Step 4: Employed bees generate new solutions based on Eq. (6), calculate their fitness values, and select the solution based on a greedy strategy. If it is a better solution, replace the previous solution.
Step 5: Calculate the probabilities of employed bees being followed based on Eq. (3).
Step 6: Onlooker bees select employed bees to follow using the roulette wheel selection rule. They search for new solutions near the selected bee based on Eq. (7), calculate the fitness value of the new solution, and choose the solution based on a greedy strategy. If it is a better solution, replace the previous solution.

Step 7: If a bee fails to find a better solution within a certain threshold, it is abandoned. Scout bees then search for better solutions based on Eq. (1).

Step 8: Record the best solution until the final condition is met and output the best solution.

These steps outline the process of the improved algorithm, which incorporates a dynamic inertia weight factor and a modified search strategy to enhance its convergence speed and search capability, while addressing the limitations of the original Artificial Bee Colony algorithm.

4   Experiment

4.1   Test Functions

To validate the effectiveness of the ABC algorithm, the experiment used eight standard test functions defined in reference [12] as fitness functions for optimization testing. These eight functions encompass four basic characteristics: unimodal separable, unimodal non-separable, multimodal separable, and multimodal non-separable. The expressions, search ranges, and theoretical optimum values for each function are shown in Table 1. Among them, f_1, f_5, and f_6 have unimodal separable properties, f_2, f_3, and f_4 have unimodal non-separable properties, f_7 has multimodal separable properties, and f_8 has multimodal non-separable properties.

4.2   Test Functions Algorithm Accuracy Comparison

This study conducted simulation experiments using MATLAB 2016b environment. In this experiment, the proposed IABC was compared with the standard ABC algorithm and the GABC algorithm. The dimensions were set to 30 and 50, respectively. The population size of bees was set to 50, the maximum iteration count was 1000, and the threshold for determining the number of times trapped in local optima was set to 100. The results were obtained as the average of 10 experiments, and the average fitness values of the functions were recorded for 10 trials. The experimental result data can be found in Table 2 and Table 3.

According to the data in Table 2, for the 30-dimensional experiments, the IABC algorithm outperformed both the standard ABC algorithm and the GABC algorithm in all tested functions except for f_5. In function f_5, both the GABC and IABC algorithms achieved the same result by finding the global optimum. The standard ABC algorithm failed to find the global optimum in all tested functions, while the GABC algorithm only found the global optimum in function f_5. On the other hand, the IABC algorithm found the global optimum in functions f_1, f_2, and f_5.

As the dimension increases, the amount of data to be processed in each iteration also increases, and the information about the global optimum becomes more complex, making the optimization process more challenging. According to the data in Table 3, with increasing dimensions, the IABC algorithm still outperforms the standard ABC and GABC algorithms in all functions. Additionally, the convergence accuracy of the standard ABC and GABC algorithms decreases significantly, while the IABC algorithm

Table 1. Test function.

Functions	Domain	Global optimum
$f_1(x) = \sum\limits_{i=1}^{D} x_i^2$	$[-100, 100]$	0
$f_2(x) = \sum\limits_{i=1}^{D} \left(\sum\limits_{j=1}^{i} x_j \right)^2$	$[-100, 100]$	0
$f_3(x) = \max\limits_{i}(|x_i| 1 \le i \le D)$	$[-100, 100]$	0
$f_4(x) = \sum\limits_{i=1}^{D-1} \left[100\left(x_{i+1} - x_i^2\right)^2 + (x_i - 1)^2 \right]$	$[-30, 30]$	0
$f_5(x) = \sum\limits_{i=1}^{D} (x_i + 0.5)^2$	$[-100, 100]$	0
$f_6(x) = \sum\limits_{i=1}^{D} ix_i^4 + \text{rand}[0, 1)$	$[-1.28, 1.28]$	0
$f_7(x) = \sum\limits_{i=1}^{D} \left[x_i^2 - 10\cos(2\pi x_i) + 10 \right]$	$[-5.12, 5.12]$	0
$f_8(x) = -20 \cdot \exp\left(-0.2 \cdot \sqrt{\dfrac{1}{D} \sum\limits_{i=1}^{D} x_i^2}\right)$ $-\exp\left(\dfrac{1}{D} \sum\limits_{i=1}^{D} \cos(2\pi x_i)\right) + 20 + e$	$[-32, 32]$	0

Table 2. Test results when dimension 30.

Functions	ABC	GABC	IABC
f_1	3.86E + 03	1.95E-35	0
f_2	4.28E + 04	4.91E-02	0
f_3	4.57E-01	6.73E + 01	1.09E-215
f_4	1.01E + 07	6.84E + 01	2.79E + 01
f_5	4.90 E + 03	0	0
f_6	3.97E + 00	6.28E-03	1.56E-05
f_7	2.69E + 02	1.09E + 02	3.46E + 01
f_8	1.26E + 01	3.97E-10	4.44E-15

maintains a relatively high level of optimization accuracy. For functions f_1, f_2, and f_5, the IABC algorithm can still converge to the global optimum fitness. The experimental

Table 3. Test results when dimension 50.

Functions	ABC	GABC	IABC
f_1	3.11E + 04	1.80E-18	0
f_2	7.21E + 04	5.91E + 03	0
f_3	8.36E + 01	8.41E + 01	4.45E-86
f_4	1.36E + 08	9.13E + 01	4.76E + 01
f_5	3.41E + 04	1	0
f_6	8.46E + 01	1.36E-02	5.50E-05
f_7	5.37E + 02	2.43E + 02	1.98E + 02
f_8	1.87E + 01	1.37E + 00	4.44E-15

results demonstrate that the IABC algorithm has clear advantages over the standard ABC and GABC algorithms in high-dimensional optimization problems.

Based on the experimental data, the IABC algorithm shows generally favorable optimization performance for functions with the four basic properties. Moreover, regardless of low or high dimensions, the proposed algorithm achieves higher search accuracy compared to the other two algorithms.

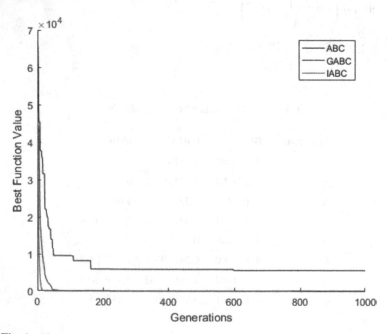

Fig. 1. The convergence of ABC, GABC and IABC on function f_1 when D = 30

4.3 Convergence Rate Comparison

To visually illustrate the search performance and convergence speed of the proposed algorithm, partial optimization curves are selected for several test functions. Figures 1, 2, 3, and 4 show the variations of the optimal function values with the number of search iterations for the functions f_1, f_2, f_7 and f_8 under the standard ABC, GABC, and IABC algorithms. These four test functions represent different basic properties, where f_1 represents unimodal separable properties, f_2 represents unimodal non-separable properties, f_7 represents multimodal separable properties and f_8 represents multimodal non-separable properties. Figures 1 and 2 depict the convergence curves for a dimension of 30, while Figs. 3 and 4 represent the convergence curves for a dimension of 50.

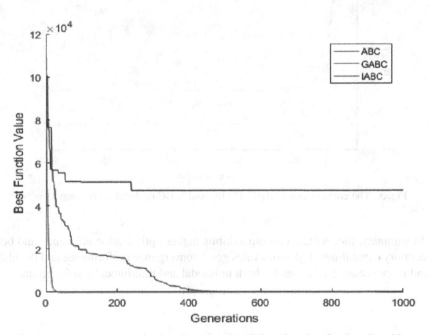

Fig. 2. The convergence of ABC, GABC and IABC on function f_2 when $D = 30$

From Fig. 1, it can be observed that when dealing with a unimodal separable function f_1, the proposed algorithm does not exhibit a significant advantage in terms of speed compared to the GABC algorithm, which also demonstrates fast convergence and accuracy. However, Fig. 2 reveals a significant improvement in convergence speed for the proposed algorithm when dealing with the unimodal non-separable function f_2.

Figures 3 and 4 demonstrate that when facing complex multimodal functions, the proposed algorithm shows significant improvements in both optimization accuracy and convergence speed. It achieves fast optimization while ensuring high accuracy. Overall, the optimal function value curves of the IABC algorithm are steeper compared to the standard ABC and GABC algorithms, indicating better search results and a noticeable improvement. The IABC algorithm consistently discovers better solutions at a faster rate.

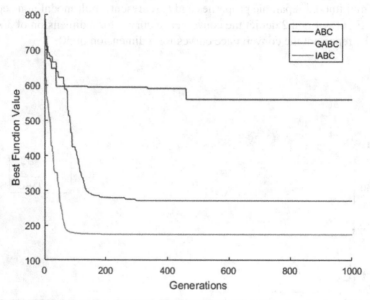

Fig. 3. The convergence of ABC, GABC and IABC on function f_7 when $D = 50$

In summary, the IABC algorithm exhibits higher optimization efficiency and better exploratory capabilities. It demonstrates good convergence performance and the ability to find more accurate solutions for both unimodal and multimodal test functions.

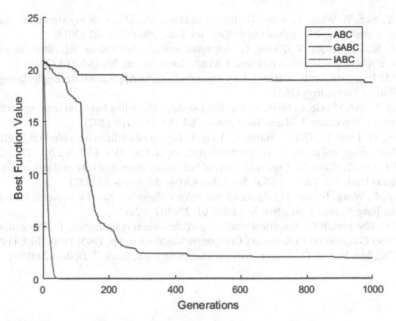

Fig. 4. The convergence of ABC, GABC and IABC on function f_8 when $D = 50$

5   Conclusion

This paper proposes an improved ABC algorithm (IABC) that introduces a dynamic inertia weight factor based on GABC. Additionally, new search strategies are employed in both the employed bee phase and the onlooker bee phase to replace the original search strategy. Experimental results demonstrate that the introduction of the dynamic inertia weight factor effectively enhances the algorithm's global search capability, preventing it from getting trapped in local optima. The improved ABC algorithm significantly accelerates the convergence speed and achieves convergence values that are closer to the global optimal values of the test functions.

Acknowledgements. This work was supported by the National Natural Science Foundation of China under Grant 62176273 and by National first-class undergraduate major in software engineering.

References

1. Karaboga, D.: An idea based on honey bee swarm for numerical optimization. Erciyes University (2005)
2. Zhang, P.: Research on Bayesian Network Structure Learning Based on Artificial Bee Colony Algorithm. Xi'an University of Electronic Science and Technology (2014)
3. Pan, X.Q., Lu, Y., Li, S.M., Li, R.X.: An improved artificial bee colony with new search strategy. Int. J. Wirel. Mob. Comput. **9**(4), 391–396 (2015)

4. Jin, Y., Sun, Y., Wang, J., Wang, D.: Improved elite artificial bee colony algorithm based on simplex method. J. Zhengzhou Univ. (Eng. Sci. Edn.) **39**(06), 36–42 (2018)
5. Chen, S., Ji, W., Qiu, Y., Zhang, G.: Improved artificial bee colony algorithm for solving flexible job-shop scheduling problem. J. Mach. Tools Autom. **05**, 161–164 (2018)
6. Su, M.: Improved Artificial Bee Colony Algorithm and Its Application Research. Zhongyuan Institute of Technology (2021)
7. Wang, Y., Ma, M., Ge, J., Miao, S.: Flexible job shop scheduling based on improved artificial bee colony algorithm. J. Mach. Tools Autom. **03**,159–163+168 (2021)
8. Zhang, H., Long, D., Qin, T., Wang, X., Yang, J.: Improved artificial bee colony algorithm for WSN coverage and connectivity optimization. Comput. Eng. Des. **43**(10), 2701–2710 (2022)
9. Ren, J., Du, Z., Wang, X.: Improved artificial bee colony algorithm for cloud task scheduling. J. Henan Univ. Sci. Technol. (Nat. Sci. Edn.) **43**(04), 55–60+6–7 (2022)
10. Wang, J., Wang, B., Ge, M.: Artificial bee colony algorithm based on reverse learning. J. Mudanjiang Normal Univ. (Nat. Sci. Edn.) **01**, 23–30 (2022)
11. Shi, Y., Eberhart, R.C.: Empirical study of particle swarm optimization. In: Proceedings of the 1999 Congress on Evolutionary Computation.Washington, pp. 1945–1950. IEEE (1999)
12. Yao, X., Liu, Y., Lin, G.: Evolutionary programming made faster. **3**(2), 0–102 (1999)

Pathological Voice Recognition Based on Multi-feature Fusion

Ruizhi Zhu[1], Ruixiang Li[1(✉)], Jiayun Li[1], Yan Liu[2], Yang Liu[3], and Jinrang Li[3]

[1] School of Information Engineering, Minzu University of China, Beijing 100081, China
ruixiang0822@163.com
[2] School of Chinese Ethnic Minority Languages and Literatures, Minzu University of China,
Beijing 100081, China
[3] College of Otolaryngology Head and Neck Surgery, The Sixth Medical Center of PLA
General Hospital, Beijing 100048, China

Abstract. Voice communication is a common mode of communication, and with
the accelerated lifestyle, the incidence of voice disorders has increased. Currently,
the classification and evaluation of pathological voice rely mainly on clinicians'
subjective hearing perception of the voice, which is influenced by subjective factors in the process of classification and evaluation. Therefore, this paper designs a
multidimensional feature vector (57 dimensions) for the voice signal by extracting
MFCC, F0, jitter, shimmer, and HNR parameters of vowel a/i. The feature vector is processed through principal component analysis (PCA) and support vector
machine (SVM) classifiers, and the classification evaluation algorithm is investi-
gated by downscaling and dimensioning the original feature matrix. The experimental study is conducted on different types of pathological and normal voice data
collected from the clinic. The results of the experiment indicate that the model in
this paper has good recognition ability for pathological voice. The classification
accuracy of normal and pathological voice reached 91.96%, and the classification
accuracy of mild and severe abnormal voice reached 82.74%. These results demonstrate the effectiveness of the automatic classification and evaluation algorithm for
pathological voice proposed in this paper.

Keywords: voice disorders · pathological voice recognition and classification ·
voice signal features · support vector machine

1 Introduction

The human voice is a crucial tool for interpersonal communication, social interaction,
and information exchange in daily life. The quality of one's voice can directly impact
their ability to express themselves verbally. Consequently, voice disorders can significantly decrease people's quality of life and productivity, affecting their communication
skills and daily tasks' performance. Unfortunately, the prevalence of voice disorders is
continuously increasing due to expanding human social interaction activities and changing lifestyles. Research suggests that between 3% and 9% of the world's population will
have varying degrees of voice disorders or symptoms. Voice disorders can result from

© The Author(s), under exclusive license to Springer Nature Switzerland AG 2023
Y. Yang et al. (Eds.): AIMS 2023, LNCS 14202, pp. 15–27, 2023.
https://doi.org/10.1007/978-3-031-45140-9_2

various factors, including vocal abuse, neurological disorders, and laryngeal cancer. Traditional methods for detecting voice disorders rely on invasive examinations of patients with testing equipment, such as electronic laryngoscopes and laryngeal electromyography. These methods require high levels of clinical experience and subjective judgment, making early diagnoses difficult, costly, and sometimes delaying treatment time. Consequently, researchers are increasingly interested in early detection and treatment of voice disorders [1]. Studies have shown that when the voice is diseased, the acoustic signals of the normal and pathological voice show deviations in acoustic parameters. Therefore, researchers can extract acoustic features that effectively distinguish between normal and pathological voices by collecting voice signals from patients with voice diseases. This enables objective assessment of voice quality using machine learning methods, which can help avoid secondary injuries that laryngoscopy may bring to patients' larynx, reduce patients' pain and medical costs, and serve as an effective diagnostic tool for doctors to diagnose voice diseases.

The application of artificial intelligence in any field requires robust databases. The quality of data in a pathological voice database directly impacts the accuracy of classification experiments. Currently, researchers mainly use three databases to study voice disease recognition: the MEEI database (Massachusetts Eye and Ear Infirmary), the German Saarbruecken Voice Database (SVD), and the Arabic Voice Pathology Database (AVPD). The MEEI database is a commercial database developed by the Massachusetts Eye and Ear Infirmary voice and speech laboratory. It contains 53 normal and 657 pathological continuous vowel /a/ voice samples. The MEEI database was the earliest dataset established in the field of pathological voice detection and classification research, and it remains the most widely used and recognized dataset. However, the MEEI database has different sampling environments and frequencies for normal and pathological voice samples, which can lead to unbalanced voice sample data [2]. The SVD database is a freely downloadable German dataset recorded by the School of Speech at Saarland University. It includes more than 2,000 normal and pathological continuous vowel sounds /a/, /i/, and /u/ voice samples. The AVPD database is an Arabic dataset established by King Saud University according to a standardized recording protocol. The AVPD database avoids the problems of the MEEI database and collects 188 normal and 178 pathological continuous vowels /a/, /i/, and /u/ voice samples [3].

Studies have shown that measurements of amplitude and frequency perturbations in the voices of African American adult males and white adult males differ [4]. Factors such as race and geography can impact individual voice characteristics. To accurately reflect the voice characteristics of the target group, we believe it's necessary to collect voice samples from the target group to build a database. This will help us find an accurate and reliable automated diagnostic solution for voice disorders. Furthermore, our current study shows that most experimental results were based on small sample data sets of tens or hundreds, and results on different data sets showed some differences. Most studies focus on dichotomous experiments to distinguish normal and pathological voices, and multiple classifications for pathological voices need further exploration.

In this paper, we explore automatic detection and classification of voice lesions using acoustic features such as Mel Frequency Cepstral Coefficient (MFCC), Fundamental Frequency (F0), Jitter, Shimmer and Harmonics-to-Noise ratio (HNR), along with machine learning methods, on a self-built clinical dataset. Our contributions are four-fold: (1) We established a large-scale Chinese pathological voice dataset, comprising more than 2000 cases of vocal cord paralysis, vocal cord cyst, vocal cord polyp, tumor, and other common pathological voice types, as well as normal voice samples of the /a/ and /i/ sounds. (2) By using a combination of features and SVM classifier, and optimizing the parameters with grid search, we developed an accurate and robust automatic classifi- cation and evaluation algorithm for pathological voices, with promising prospects for auxiliary diagnosis. (3) We conducted comparative experiments on the voice samples of continuous vowels /a/ and /i/ separately, and found that continuous vowel /a/ outper- formed continuous vowel /i/ in this method. (4) We explored pathological classification by first identifying four common pathological voices: vocal cord paralysis, vocal cord cyst, vocal cord polyp, and tumor, and then dividing all pathological voices into mildly abnormal and severely abnormal, for a binary classification experiment. The experiment resulted in good classification performance in distinguishing between mildly abnormal and severely abnormal pathological voices.

2 Related Work

The identification and classification of pathological voices remains a challenging area in speech detection research. In recent years, researchers have focused on using various methods and techniques to detect voice disorders, exploring numerous feature param- eters and recognition machines with strong classification ability. Commonly extracted features include entropy, energy, mel frequency cepstrum coefficient, cepstrum domain, frequency, sub-noise ratio, short-term cepstrum parameters, normalized noise energy, and more [5]. Following feature extraction, the classification task is performed using various machine learning methods, including K-means clustering, decision trees, Gaus- sian mixture models, support vector machines, and more [6]. However, most studies have been limited to distinguishing between normal and pathological voices, neglect- ing the identification of different pathological voices, and experiments have often been conducted on small sample datasets.

[7] utilized the inverse filtering method to extract voice gate signal parameters, selecting 34 normal voice samples and 34 pathological voice samples as the dataset in the SVD database. Binary classification experiments were conducted using support vector machine (SVM) and k-nearest neighbor (k-NN) classifiers, with experimental results indicating an accuracy of 98.5% for SVM and 88.2% for k-NN. In [8], DBSCAN was proposed for detecting voice disorders, with 53 normal voice samples and 173 pathological voice samples selected as the dataset in the MEEI database. A support vector machine was used as a classifier, achieving the highest accuracy of 98%. In [9], MFCC features were extracted from 60 normal voice samples and 40 pathological voice samples, with SVM and GMM classifiers used to dichotomize voice signals into normal and pathological categories. The highest accuracy of 96.5% was achieved. In [10], 60 normal voice samples and 402 pathological voice samples were collected and datasets were created separately based on gender. MFCC features were extracted and used for dichotomous classification experiments with SVM and GMM classifiers. Results showed that the overall accuracy of female voice samples was lower than that of male samples.

On male samples, SVM achieved the highest accuracy of 92.24% and GMM achieved the highest accuracy of 89.00%. On female samples, SVM achieved a maximum accuracy of 85.18% and GMM achieved a maximum accuracy of 83.56%. In [11], a convolutional neural network (CNN) was applied for pathological voice recognition, with 150 normal voice samples and 150 pathological voice samples selected as the dataset in the SVD database. ResNet34 was chosen as the convolutional neural network model, achieving the highest accuracy of 95.41% in normal and pathological voice binary classification experiments.

3 Materials and Methods

This study aims to explore the extraction of effective and accurate pathological voice feature parameters using acoustic analysis for pathological voice assessment. The high redundancy of the original voice signal necessitates the use of feature extraction and pattern recognition, combined with efficient classifiers, for automatic recognition and objective assessment of pathological voice.

In this paper, we focus on extracting MFCC, F0, Jitter, Shimmer, and HNR features. Voice quality is affected by the frequency, amplitude, energy, and resonance peaks of vocal fold vibration and resonance cavity modulation. MFCC features capture frequency and energy changes in audio signals, providing valuable information for audio classification tasks and identifying the extent of laryngeal lesions. F0, Jitter, Shimmer and HNR are statistical characteristics extracted directly from the sound pressure signal and can reflect the laryngeal pathology to some extent.

The fusion of these features forms the input vector for the classifier. In the final implementation, a support vector machine was used as the classifier to distinguish normal and pathological voice samples, as well as classify pathological voice samples into mild and severe abnormalities.

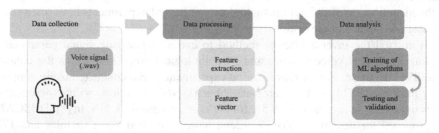

Fig. 1. The block diagram for the pathological voice classification

Figure 1 depicts the flow of the whole task, we first performed the data collection work by storing all voice sample files in wav format. Then the voice samples were feature extracted and our proposed MPGS (Multi-features-PCA-GridSearchCV-SVM) method was used to achieve automatic classification and evaluation of pathological voices.

3.1 Database

The Chinese pathological voice samples used in this study were obtained from the College of Otolaryngology Head and Neck Surgery at The Sixth Medical Center of PLA General Hospital, with collaborative authorization. The Chinese normal voice samples were collected in an indoor environment without noise interference from normal individuals without recent laryngeal diseases under the guidance of professional physicians. The sampling time for each sample was between 1.5 to 3 s, and the sampling frequency was 16 kHz. Specifically, the voice samples were collected for the Chinese vowels /a/ and /i/.

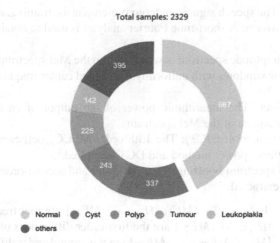

Fig. 2. Distribution of normal and voice disorder samples in the database

A total of 2329 voice samples were collected, including 987 normal voice samples and 1342 pathological voice samples. Among them, the pathological voice samples included common voice diseases such as cysts, polyps, white spots, palsy, nodules, tumors, and spasmodic dysphonia. Figure 2 shows the distribution of normal and pathological voice samples in the database.

3.2 Feature Extraction

Feature extraction is the first step to build a voice disease recognition system. There are many traditional acoustic feature parameters used for voice analysis and recognition, and some results have been achieved in the detection and diagnosis of voice pathology. In this experiment, MFCC, F0, Jitter, Shimmer and HNR features, which are widely used in clinical medical detection of pathological voice, were selected. When laryngeal pathology occurs, these feature parameters deviate from normal values, thus allowing effective identification of normal and pathological voice samples.

MFCC is one of the most commonly used features in speech recognition and speaker identification. It takes into account the nonlinear nature of human hearing by first mapping a linear spectrum into a nonlinear spectrum based on the Mel-scale of human auditory perception and then converting it to the inverse spectral domain [12]. Its main advantage is that it does not require prior pitch estimation, which is a problem commonly faced by most acoustic parameters in the prior art. Since such features do not depend on the nature of the signal and are consistent with the human auditory model, they have better robustness [13]. The MFCC feature extraction algorithm is shown in Eq. (1).

$$Mel(f) = 2595lg(1 + \frac{f}{700}) \tag{1}$$

where f represents the actual frequency of the sound signal in Hz.

The MFCC feature calculation process is described as follows:

- Pre-processing: The speech signals undergo pre-emphasis, framing, and windowing.
- Fast Fourier transform: A short-time Fourier analysis is used to obtain the amplitude spectrum.
- Mel filter: The amplitude spectrum is wrapped into the Mel spectrum using 24 overlapping triangular windows with uniformly distributed center frequencies of the Mel scale windows.
- Logarithmic power: The logarithmic power of the output of each filter bank is calculated as the square of the Mel spectrum.
- Discrete cosine transform (DCT): The 13th order MFCC coefficients are obtained using the logarithmic power method and DCT is applied.
- Perform inverse spectrum boosting: The first-order and second-order differences of the MFCCs are extracted.

$\forall MF_i \in R, i = 1, 2, \ldots, 39$, $\{MF_1, MF_2, \cdots, MF_{13}\}$ are mel frequency cepstral coefficient, $\{MF_{14}, MF_{15}, \cdots, MF_{26}\}$ are the first-order differences of mel frequency cepstral coefficient, $\{MF_{27}, MF_{28}, \cdots, MF_{39}\}$ are the second-order differences of mel frequency cepstral coefficient.

Defining $MFCC \in R^{1 \times 39}$, the MFCC feature vector is described by the following equation:

$$MFCC = \{MF_1, MF_2, \cdots, MF_{39}\} \tag{2}$$

Jitter belongs to the class of fundamental frequency parameters and is related to the fundamental frequency value. Therefore, the accuracy of F0 extraction directly affects the extraction of Jitter parameters.

Fundamental frequency (F0) refers to the frequency of vocal fold vibration during speech production and is widely used in speech recognition and detection. The extraction of fundamental frequency from speech signals is usually performed using the autocorrelation function method [14]. The value of fundamental frequency depends on the pressure and tension of the vocal folds. The higher the pressure or tension, the higher the fundamental frequency. When the vocal folds are affected by a disease, changes in their length, thickness, and shape can result in improper closure and asymmetric vibration, leading to variations in the fundamental frequency and affecting the acoustic characteristics of the speech signal.

Defining $Pitch \in R^{1 \times 5}$, the F0 feature vector is described by the following equation:

$$Pitch = \{Pit_1, Pit_2, \cdots, Pit_5\} \tag{3}$$

where Pit_1 is the median of F0, Pit_2 is the mean of F0, Pit_3 is the standard deviation of F0, Pit_4 is the minimum of F0, Pit_5 is the maximum of F0.

Jitter [15] refers to the variation in frequency between adjacent speech signal cycles. Patients with a lack of control over vocal fold vibration tend to have higher jitter values. Jitter can be calculated using the following Eq. (4):

$$Jitter = \frac{\frac{1}{N}\sum_{i=1}^{N-1}|F_i - F_{i+1}|}{\frac{1}{N}\sum_{i=1}^{N}F_i} \tag{4}$$

where Fi is the frequency of the signal in the ith pronunciation period and N is the number of periods.

On this basis, further calculations are made to obtain Jitter (local), Jitter (rap), Jitter (ppq5), and Jitter (ddp). Jitter (local) is calculated as the average absolute difference between consecutive periods, divided by the average period. Jitter (rap) is calculated as the Relative Average Perturbation, the average absolute difference between a period and the average of it and its two neighbours, divided by the average period. Jitter (ppq5) is calculated as the five-point Period Perturbation Quotient, the average absolute difference between a period and the average of it and its four closest neighbours, divided by the average period. Jitter (ddp) is calculated as the average absolute difference between consecutive differences between consecutive periods, divided by the average period.

Defining $Jit \in R^{1 \times 4}$, the Jitter feature vector is described by the following equation:

$$Jit = \{Jit_1, Jit_2, Jit_3, Jit_4\} \tag{5}$$

where Jit_1 is the Jitter(local), Jit_2 is the Jitter(rap), Jit_3 is the Jitter(ppq5), Jit_4 is the Jitter(ddp).

Shimmer [15] refers to the variation in amplitude between adjacent speech signal cycles. A decrease in vocal fold resistance can lead to a change in the amplitude of vocal fold cycles associated with breathing and vocalization, resulting in an increase in Shimmer. Shimmer is calculated using the following Eq. (6):

$$Shimmer = \frac{\frac{1}{N-1}\sum_{i=1}^{N-1}|A_i - A_{i+1}|}{\frac{1}{N}\sum_{i=1}^{N}A_i} \tag{6}$$

where A_i is the frequency of the signal in the ith pronunciation period and N is the number of periods.

On this basis, further calculations are made to obtain Shimmer (local), Shimmer (local dB), Shimmer (apq3), Shimmer (apq5), Shimmer (apq11), Shimmer (ddp). Shimmer (local) is calculated as the average absolute difference between the amplitudes of consecutive periods, divided by the average amplitude. Shimmer (local dB) is calculated as the average absolute base-10 logarithm of the difference between the amplitudes of consecutive periods, multiplied by 20. Shimmer (apq3) is calculated as the three-point Amplitude Perturbation Quotient, the average absolute difference between the amplitude of a period and the average of the amplitudes of its neighbours, divided by the average amplitude. Shimmer (apq5) is calculated as the five-point Amplitude Perturbation Quotient, the average absolute difference between the amplitude of a period and the average of the amplitudes of it and its four closest neighbours, divided by the average amplitude. Shimmer (apq11) is calculated as the 11-point Amplitude Perturbation Quotient, the average absolute difference between the amplitude of a period and the average of the amplitudes of it and its ten closest neighbours, divided by the average amplitude. Shimmer (ddp) is calculated as the average absolute difference between consecutive differences between the amplitudes of consecutive periods.

Defining $Shim \in R^{1 \times 6}$, the Shimmer feature vector is described by the following equation:

$$Shim = \{Shim_1, Shim_2, \cdots, Shim_6\} \tag{7}$$

where $Shim_1$ is the Shimmer (local), $Shim_2$ is the Shimmer (local dB), $Shim_3$ is the Shimmer (apq3), $Shim_4$ is the Shimmer (apq5), $Shim_5$ is the Shimmer (apq11), $Shim_6$ is the Shimmer (ddp).

HNR is the ratio of harmonic and noise components in the voice. It is an objective indicator for detecting pathological voice and evaluating voice quality, and can effectively reflect the vocal fold closure. HNR is calculated as shown in Eq. (8).

$$HNR = 10 \times \log_{10} \frac{E_{harmonics}}{E_{noise}} \tag{8}$$

where $E_{harmonics}$ is the harmonic component energy and E_{noise} is the noise component energy.

Defining $H \in R^{1 \times 3}$, the HNR feature vector is described by the following equation:

$$H = \{H_1, H_2, H_3\} \tag{9}$$

where H_1 is the Harmonicity (Mean_autocorrelation), H_2 is the Harmonicity (Mean noise-to-harmonics ratio), H_3 is the Harmonicity (Mean harmonics-to-noise ratio dB).

Let V be the feature vector formed by the combination of multiple features, $V \in R^{1 \times 57}$, then V is defined as:

$$V = \{MFCC, Pitch, Jit, Shim, H\} \tag{10}$$

where $MFCC$ are the MFCC eigenvectors, $Pitch$ are the F0 eigenvectors, Jit are the Jitter eigenvectors, $Shim$ are the Shimmer eigenvectors, H are the HNR eigenvectors.

3.3 Principal Components Analysis

PCA is a commonly used data analysis method that transforms the original data into a set of linearly independent representations for each dimension through a linear transformation. This technique is useful for extracting the main feature components of the data and can be applied to combined feature vectors to extract more category information compared to single feature vectors [16]. However, it is essential to note that more feature vectors do not always lead to better results. In fact, a high number of feature dimensions can result in redundant information, which can negatively affect recognition judgment results. To address this issue, we used PCA to reduce the dimensionality of the combined feature set, eliminate redundant information, and obtain new combined features. The value of k was determined by calculating the cumulative variance contribution, and the threshold was set at 85%.

3.4 Support Vector Machine

Support vector machines (SVM) are supervised learning models that have been widely used for multi-class classification problems [17]. SVMs have good generalization capabilities for out-of-sample data, and the selection of classification thresholds can be flexibly achieved based on kernel functions [18]. In this study, we employ the radial basis function (RBF) as the kernel function of the support vector machine for the detection and classification of pathological voices.

RBF is less restrictive compared to other kernel functions and more general than the linear kernel. To find the penalty coefficient (C) and the kernel parameters (γ), a grid search method is used.

4 Experiments and Discussions

4.1 10-Fold Cross-Validation

To train and evaluate the performance of the model and to overcome the overfitting problem of the model, we used a 10-fold cross-validation method. The normal and pathological samples were proportionally divided into 10 equally sized sample subsets, and one sample subset was used each time as the validation set, and the remaining 9 subsets were used as the training set. The average of the 10 assessment metrics was used as the final assessment metric.

4.2 Evaluation Metrics

In this paper, we use the Accuracy, Precision, Recall and F1 Score based assessment model [19]. Equations (11), (12), (13), (14) describe the calculation of Accuracy, Precision, Recall and F1 Score metrics.

$$\mathrm{Accuracy} = \frac{TP + TN}{TP + TN + FP + FN} \tag{11}$$

$$\mathrm{Precision} = \frac{TP}{TP + FP} \tag{12}$$

$$\mathrm{Recall} = \frac{TP}{TP + FN} \tag{13}$$

$$\mathrm{F1Score} = 2 \times \frac{\mathrm{Precision} \times \mathrm{Recall}}{\mathrm{Precision} + \mathrm{Recall}} \tag{14}$$

4.3 Results

We believe that a single feature parameter vector contains only a part of the information in the voice signal and ignores many other useful pieces of information. This could result in the inability to distinguish normal and pathological noise effectively. Combining each

single feature parameter vector into a feature set can obtain the characteristics of pathological voice more comprehensively, thereby improving the performance of the model
in distinguishing normal and pathological voice. To test this hypothesis, we conducted
ablation experiments for the feature parameters, and Table 1 shows the accuracy of
individual features, combined features, and PCA reduced feature sets in distinguishing
normal and pathological voice samples on vowel /a/ and vowel /i/ voice samples. The
results demonstrate that the processed feature sets can distinguish normal and pathological voices more effectively on vowel /a/ and vowel /i/ voice samples compared to
individual and combined features.

Table 1. Comparison of different parameters in the recognition of voice pathology

Vowel	Classification	Parameter	Accuracy(%)
/a/	normal × pathology	F0	80.29
		jitter	61.57
		shimmer	63.03
		HNR	67.35
		MFCC	76.62
		combination	87.24
		MPGS	**91.96**
/i/	normal × pathology	F0	72.73
		jitter	55.81
		shimmer	51.33
		HNR	59.12
		MFCC	71.18
		combination	79.04
		MPGS	**83.85**

Table 2 displays the performance of the processed feature set on vowel/a/ and vowel/i/
voice samples. The results indicate that the processed feature set outperforms individual
and combined features in distinguishing normal and pathological voices on both vowel/a/
and vowel/i/ voice samples.

Further experiments were conducted to subclassify different pathological voices
using the processed feature set and vowel/a/ voice samples. Four common pathological
voices, paralysis, cyst, polyp, and tumor, were selected for the subclassification experiments. The pathological voice samples were divided into mild and severe abnormalities, and experiments were performed to distinguish mild abnormalities from severe
abnormalities. Table 3 presents the results of these experiments, demonstrating that the
model can perform rank subclassification for pathological voice effectively.

To demonstrate the feasibility of our proposed method, we compared it with some
research works that have larger total sample sizes. Table 4 illustrates the comparison

Table 2. Comparison of different vowels in the recognition of voice pathology

Vowel	Classification	Accuracy (%)	Precision (%)	Recall (%)	F1 Score (%)
/a/	normal × pathology	91.96	90.72	91.95	91.33
/i/	normal × pathology	83.85	89.73	76.28	82.46

Table 3. Comparison of different pathologies in the subdivision

Vowel	Classification	Accuracy (%)	Precision (%)	Recall (%)	F1 Score (%)
/a/	paralysis × cyst	67.75	70.16	66.31	68.18
	paralysis × polyp	63.93	59.72	60.49	60.10
	paralysis × tumor	70.27	76.83	68.52	72.43
	cyst × polyp	68.51	70.64	65.98	68.23
	cyst × tumor	72.39	81.01	69.43	74.77
	polyp × tumor	76.52	74.61	73.75	74.17
	light × serious	82.74	89.70	76.22	82.41

Table 4. Comparison of different methods in the recognition of voice pathology

Classification	Method	Accuracy(%)
normal × pathology	[2]	92.79
	[20]	85.77
	MPGS	**91.96**
G0 × G1 × G2 × G3	[21]	80.58
light × serious	**MPGS**	**82.74**

results. [2] used combined features of peak and lag and entropy to classify 266 normal voice samples and 263 pathological voice samples with vowel /a/ from the SVD database, achieving slightly higher accuracy than ours on normal and pathological dichotomous classification. [20] used a dataset of 685 normal voice samples and 685 pathological voice samples with vowel/a/ and selected features similar to ours, but our method's treatment of combined features and model training improvements led to higher accuracy on normal and pathological dichotomization. [21] classified vowel/a/ pathological voice samples into four classes according to GRBAS by hoarseness G and performed a four-classification experiment, achieving a classification accuracy of 80.58%.

5 Conclusion and Future Work

This paper presents experiments on the recognition of normal and pathological voices, as well as the subclassification of pathological voices. The approach involves utilizing various features extracted from speech signals corresponding to normal and pathological voice samples for classification, with the aim of developing an effective diagnostic model to aid physicians in decision-making. The results demonstrate that the SVM model is capable of effectively distinguishing between normal and pathological voice samples with an average accuracy of 91.6% when using MFCC, F0, jitter, shimmer, and HNR features. Additionally, the model showed potential for pathological subclassification experiments, achieving an average accuracy of 82.74%. In future work, we plan to expand our dataset and explore new feature extraction methods for specific pathological voice recognition and subclassification experiments.

References

1. Markaki, M., Stylianou, Y.: Voice pathology detection and discrimination based on modulation spectral features. IEEE Trans. Audio Speech Lang. Process. **19**(7), 1938–1948 (2011)
2. Al-Nasheri, A., et al.: Voice pathology detection and classification using auto-correlation and entropy features in different frequency regions. IEEE Access **6**, 6961–6974 (2018)
3. Mesallam, T.A., et al.: Development of the Arabic voice pathology database and its evaluation by using speech features and machine learning algorithms. J. Healthc. Eng. **2017**, 1–13 (2017)
4. Walton, J.H., Orlikoff, R.F.: Speaker race identification from acoustic cues in the vocal signal. J. Speech Lang. Hear. Res. **37**(4), 738–745 (1994)
5. Dubuisson, T., Dutoit, T., Gosselin, B., Remacle, M.: On the use of the correlation between acoustic descriptors for the normal/pathological voices discrimination. EURASIP J. Adv. Signal Process. **2009**(1), 173967 (2009)
6. Al-Dhief, F.T., et al.: A survey of voice pathology surveillance systems based on internet of things and machine learning algorithms. IEEE Access **8**, 64514–64533 (2020)
7. Mittal, V., Sharma, R.K.: Glottal signal analysis for voice pathology. In: 2019 2nd International Conference on Innovations in Electronics, Signal Processing and Communication (IESC), Shillong, India, pp. 54–59, March 2019
8. Amami, R., Smiti, A.: An incremental method combining density clustering and support vector machines for voice pathology detection. Comput. Electr. Eng. **57**, 257–265 (2017)
9. Amara, F., Fezari, M., Bourouba, H.: An improved GMM-SVM system based on distance metric for voice pathology detection. Appl. Math. Inf. Sci. **10**(3), 1061–1070 (2016)
10. Fang, S.-H., et al.: Detection of pathological voice using cepstrum vectors: a deep learning approach. J. Voice **33**(5), 634–641 (2019)
11. Mohammed, M.A., et al.: Voice pathology detection and classification using convolutional neural network model. Appl. Sci. **10**(11), 3723 (2020)
12. Reddy, M.K., Alku, P.: A comparison of cepstral features in the detection of pathological voices by varying the input and filterbank of the cepstrum computation. IEEE Access **9**, 135953–135963 (2021)

13. Albadr, M.A.A., Tiun, S., Ayob, M., Mohammed, M., AL-Dhief, F.T.: Mel-frequency cepstral coefficient features based on standard deviation and principal component analysis for language identification systems. Cogn. Comput. **13**(5), 1136–1153 (2021)

14. Puts, D.A., et al.: Sexual selection on male vocal fundamental frequency in humans and other anthropoids. Proc. R. Soc. B Biol. Sci. **283**(1829), 20152830 (2016)

15. Akif Kiliç, M., Öğüt, F., Dursun, G., Okur, E., Yildirim, I., Midilli, R.: The effects of vowels on voice perturbation measures. J. Voice **18**(3), 318–324 (2004)

16. Abdi, H., Williams, L.J.: Principal component analysis. WIREs Comput. Stat. **2**(4), 433–459 (2010)

17. Cervantes, J., Garcia-Lamont, F., Rodríguez-Mazahua, L., Lopez, A.: A comprehensive survey on support vector machine classification: applications, challenges and trends. Neurocomputing **408**, 189–215 (2020)

18. Chang, C.-C., Lin, C.-J.: LIBSVM: a library for support vector machines. ACM Trans. Intell. Syst. Technol. **2**(3), 1–27 (2011)

19. Harar, P., Galaz, Z., Alonso-Hernandez, J.B., Mekyska, J., Burget, R., Smekal, Z.: Towards robust voice pathology detection: investigation of supervised deep learning, gradient boosting, and anomaly detection approaches across four databases. Neural Comput. Appl. **32**(20), 15747–15757 (2020)

20. Verde, L., De Pietro, G., Sannino, G.: Voice disorder identification by using machine learning techniques. IEEE Access **6**, 16246–16255 (2018)

21. Wang, Z., Yu, P., Yan, N., Wang, L., Ng, M.L.: Automatic assessment of pathological voice quality using multidimensional acoustic analysis based on the GRBAS scale. J. Signal Process. Syst. **82**(2), 241–251 (2016)

A Generative Model for Structured Sentiment Analysis

Yihui Li, Yice Zhang, Yifan Yang, and Ruifeng Xu[✉]

Harbin Institute of Technology, Shenzhen, China
xuruifeng@hit.edu.cn

Abstract. Structured Sentiment Analysis (SSA) aims to extract the complete sentiment structure from a given text. Existing approaches predominantly rely on the interactions of words to predict the relationships between sentiment elements. While these methods have shown effectiveness, they overlook the rich label semantics associated with SSA tasks and necessitate extensive task-specific designs. In order to address the above problems, we propose a generative framework for tackling the SSA task. We designed two templates to transform the SSA task into a text generation problem, which facilitate the training process by formulating the SSA task as a text generation problem. Through experiments conducted on three SSA datasets, we demonstrate that our proposed generative approach outperforms all existing methods, thereby highlighting the advantages of employing the generative model for SSA.

Keywords: structured sentiment analysis · sequence-to-sequence modeling

1 Introduction

The purpose of Structured Sentiment Analysis (SSA) is to comprehensively extract people's perceptions of ideas, products, or policies from a given text and organize them into a sentiment structure quadruplet (h, t, e, p), comprising the sentiment holder, target, expression, and polarity [3]. This quadruplet serves as a comprehensive abstraction, encapsulating the holder's expressed sentiment towards the target and its corresponding polarity. In comparison to other sentiment analysis tasks, SSA presents greater challenges due to the intricate relationships among the extracted sentiment elements. Moreover, effectively modeling sentiment elements consisting of multiple words, which constitutes a vital aspect of SSA, poses difficulties.

The SSA task can be divided into several subtasks, such as sentiment expression extraction, sentiment holder and sentiment target extraction, as well as relationship prediction and sentiment polarity classification. Previous studies on information extraction have used pipeline methods to first extract sentiment element spans from texts and then perform relationship prediction. Katiyar et al. [4] propose a BiLSTM-CRF model to predict sentiment elements in texts, while

Y. Yang et al. (Eds.): AIMS 2023, LNCS 14202, pp. 28–38, 2023.
https://doi.org/10.1007/978-3-031-45140-9_3

Xia et al. [14] propose a unified text span-based model to jointly extract spans and relationships. Barnes et al. [3] argue that dividing SSA into sub-tasks has become counterproductive. Therefore, they propose a unified method for SSA. This approach transforms the task into a dependency graph parsing problem and predicts all components of the sentiment structure in a unified manner.

In general, Most approaches model SSA as either a sentence-level classification task or a token-level classification task [8, 15]. These methods treat sentiment polarity labels solely as predefined categories and do not utilize the semantic information inherent in the labels, which can hinder further performance improvement. For instance, during training, a model that recognizes "delicious" as an adjective to describe food and "pasta" as a food item is more likely to grasp the relationship between them. Similarly, the sentiment polarity label associated with the sentiment structure carries semantic information, enabling the model to better predict the corresponding sentiment expression when aware that "positive" denotes a positive sentiment.

Taking inspiration from recent successes in formulating various language understanding problems, such as named entity recognition, question answering, and text classification, as generation tasks [2, 5, 7], we propose a generative method for SSA. To fully leverage the rich label semantics, our model incorporates natural language labels into the target output. Furthermore, this generative model offers efficiency advantages, as it only requires modifying the design of the label sequences for different subtasks within SSA, instead of customizing dedicated network models.

To implement a sequence-to-sequence approach for SSA, we design two templates: the natural language template and the tuple sequence template. These templates transform the original task into a sequence generation task. The target sentence generated using the natural language template represents a piece of natural language text corresponding to the given sentiment quadruplet. In this way, the SSA task becomes similar to the pre-training task of the pre-trained model, enabling the model to better leverage the knowledge within the pre-trained model during fine-tuning. On the other hand, the target sentence generated using the tuple sequence template consists of a sequence of tuples spliced by special symbols. This formulation simplifies the decoding process and allows for additional constraints to be applied during decoding.

Our paper presents the following key contributions: 1) We tackle SSA tasks in a novel generative manner; 2) We introduce two paradigms that formulate each task as a generation problem, along with a prediction normalization strategy to refine the generated outputs; 3) We conduct extensive experiments on multiple benchmark datasets, demonstrating that our approach consistently outperforms previous baselines in almost all cases.

2 Methodology

2.1 Problem Statement

Given a sentence x, SSA aims to predict all structured sentiment quadruplets $\{(h, t, e, p)\}$ corresponding to the sentiment holder h, sentiment target t, sentiment expression e and sentiment polarity p, respectively. Here, h, t, and e are typically text spans in x, while h and t could also be null if they are not explicitly mentioned. p belongs to one of the sentiment classes $\{POS, NEU, NEG\}$, representing positive, neutral, and negative sentiment, respectively.

2.2   SSA as Sequence Generation

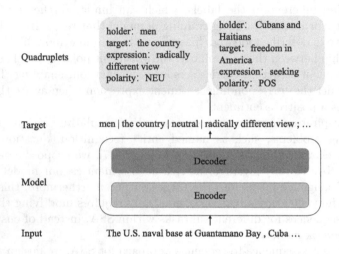

Fig. 1. Overview of the generative model for SSA.

In order to address SSA task, we propose a novel sequence-to-sequence modeling paradigm that transforms the problem into a sequence generation task. As illustrated in the Fig. 1, our approach involves using an encoder-decoder model to generate a target sequence y based on the input sentence x. This target sequence contains all of the essential structured sentiment elements required to make accurate predictions about sentiment holder, target, expression, and polarity. The structured sentiment quadruplets $Q = \{(h, t, e, p)\}$ can then be extracted from y to make predictions. To implement a sequence-to-sequence SSA approach, we design two sequence templates to transform the original task into a sequence generation task, which are the natural language template and the tuple sequence template.

2.3   Natural Language Template

Given an input text x and a sentiment structure quadruplet Q, the natural language template-based target sequence generation method converts the sentiment structure quadruplet Q into a natural language text y. On the one hand the semantic information in the sentiment structure quadruplet Q can be fully exploited in the natural language form generated in the natural language text

y. On the other hand, as both the input and target are natural language texts, the rich pre-training knowledge within the pre-trained generative model can be naturally utilized during the fine-tuning stage.

In the SSA dataset, in each sentiment structure quadruplet, expression and polarity are not missing, while holder and target may be missing. For the above cases, four natural language templates are designed, as shown in Table 1.

Table 1. Natural language template.

Type of sentiment structure	Template
(h, t, e, p)	h THINK t IS p BECAUSE e
(t, e, p)	t IS p BECAUSE e
(h, e, p)	h THINK p BECAUSE e
(e, p)	p BECAUSE e

This paradigm uses capitalised connectives to connect the above sentiment elements, this is to avoid misleading subsequent decoding steps caused by the presence of connectives in the sentiment elements. For texts containing multiple sentiment structure quadruples, we first construct target phrases for each quadruple using the template above, then splice the phrases using the ";" notation to obtain the final target sequence.

Some of the studies [16] used some pronouns to fill in the missing sentiment elements, e.g. for the sentiment structure (t, e, p): (pasta, so delicious, positive), this strategy replaced the missing sentiment holder with "Someone" and then transforms it into the target sequence "Someone THINK pasta IS positive BECAUSE so delicious". We argue that the introduction of pronouns may be misleading for subsequent decoding, as in the example above, "Someone" may also be the sentiment holder of some sentiment structure quadruplets, which the model is unable to distinguish during the decoding process.

Table 2 shows examples of target sequences constructed using natural language templates for different cases. The examples show that the output target sequences are not necessarily fluent natural language text, but the semantic information in the connectives can still be useful for extracting sentiment structure.

Table 2. Examples of target sequences constructed using natural language templates.

Sentiment structure type	Input text	Output text
(h, t, e, p)	I was very disapointed by the breakfast services	I THINK the breakfast services IS negative BECAUSE disapointed
(t, e, p)	My room was very clean	My room IS positive BECAUSE very clean
(h, e, p)	If we view this warning against the background that Putin 's government has always seen Usama Bin Ladin 's hands	we THINK negative BECAUSE this warning
(e, p)	The President 's ability to keep hope is shrinking	negative BECAUSE is shrinking

2.4   Tuple Sequence Template

The previous subsection introduced a paradigm for generating target sequences using natural language templates, which can make effective use of the semantic information in target sequences. However, the above-mentioned templates also have certain drawbacks. On the one hand, target sequences constructed using natural language templates are more complicated in the subsequent decoding steps. On the other hand, the method of generating target sequences based on natural language templates is not flexible enough, and the natural language templates need to be redesigned when additional information in the comment text needs to be extracted. For this reason, we propose a tuple sequence template.

Table 3. Tuple sequence template.

Type of sentiment structure	Template
(h, t, e, p)	h|t|p|e
(t, e, p)	null|t|p|e
(h, e, p)	h|null|p|e
(e, p)	null|null|p|e

Specifically, this template uses a certain sentiment element separator to separate different sentiment elements within the same sentiment structure and another different sentiment structure separator to separate different sentiment structures generated within the same sentence. We choose "|" as the sentiment element separator and ";" as the sentiment structure separator. In addition, for the case of missing sentiment elements of sentiment structure, we choose to use "null" to fill in the missing values.

For the four sentiment structure cases, the tuple sequence templates are shown in Table 3. For the examples in Table 2 in the previous section, target sequences constructed using the tuple sequence template are shown in Table 4. As can be seen from the Table 4, although the sequences constructed using the tuple sequence template do not have a natural language-like form, the outputs are more concise and intuitive.

Table 4. A sample sequence constructed from the tuple sequence template.

Sentiment structure type	Input text	Output text
(h, t, e, p)	I was very disapointed by the breakfast services	I|the breakfast services|negative|disapointed
(t, e, p)	My room was very clean	null|My room|positive|very clean
(h, e, p)	If we view this warning against the background that Putin 's government has always seen Usama Bin Ladin 's hands	we|null|negative|this warning
(e, p)	The President 's ability to keep hope is shrinking	null|null|negative|is shrinking

2.5   Sequence-to-Sequence Learning

We use classical encoder-decoder models to model input to target generation, such as the Transformer [11] architecture. Given a piece of input text x, the encoder of the generative model first transforms it into a context-encoded sequence e. Based on the above context-encoded sequence e, the decoder computes the target generating sequence y parameterized by the conditional probability distribution $p_\theta(y \mid e)$.

The ith output y_i of the decoder depends on the contextual encoding sequence e and the previous outputs $y_i = f_{\text{dec}}(e, y_{<i})$ where $f_{\text{dec}}(\cdot)$ denotes the decoder computations.To obtain the probability distribution for the next token, a softmax function is then applied:

$$p_\theta\left(y_{i+1} \mid e, y_{<i+1}\right) = \text{softmax}\left(W^T y_i\right) \tag{1}$$

where the W matrix maps the predicted y_i to a log vector and the softmax function is used to calculate the probability distribution over the entire set of words.

Training. With a pretrained encoder-decoder model such as T5 [9], we fine-tune the parameter weights θ by maximizing the log-likelihood $\log p_\theta(y \mid e)$:

$$\max_\theta \log p_\theta(y \mid e) = \max_\theta \sum_{i=1}^{n} \log p_\theta\left(y_i \mid e, y_{<i}\right) \tag{2}$$

where n is the length of the target sequence y.

Inference and Quad Decoding. In the prediction phase, the model generates the target sequences by means of auto regression. In the sequence decoding stage, for different target sequence templates, we design the corresponding decoding methods.

For natural language templates, the method first splits the output text sequence according to the separator ";" to obtain a series of sub-sequences. The sub-sequences is then segmented using the corresponding connectives to obtain the individual sentiment elements of the sentiment structure. Since the sentiment expressions and sentiment polarities in the sentiment structure are not missing, rules need to be designed to filter out the sentiment structures that do not meet this condition in the prediction results. Specifically, sub-sequences that do not contain the "THINK" connective are filtered out directly in the decoding process.

The simplicity of the tuple sequence template based approach is fully reflected in the decoding process. The output text sequence is first split according to the separator ";" to obtain a series of sub-sequences. For each sub-sequence, if the number of "|" is not equal to 3, the model automatically filters this sub-sequence. Each text span then automatically corresponds to the sentiment holder, sentiment target, sentiment expression and sentiment polarity of the sentiment structure quadruplet by dividing the sub-sequence with the separator "|"

3 Experiments

3.1 Experimental Setup

Datasets. We evaluate our model on three structured sentiment datasets including OpeNER [1], MPQA [12], and DS_unis [10]. The statistics of them are show in Table 5.

Evaluation Metrics. We adopt Sentiment Graph F1 (SF1) [3] score as the main evaluation metrics for all tasks. For SF1, a true positive is defined as an exact match at graph-level, weighting the overlap in predicted and gold spans for each element, averaged across all three spans. We also report the precision (P) and recall (R) scores.

Table 5. Data statistics for the SSA task.

Dataset	Train				Test			
	sentence	expression	target	holder	sentence	expression	target	holder
OpeNER	1596	2644	2471	247	399	628	572	68
MPQA	6333	1813	1576	1506	1584	427	364	293
DS_unis	1978	693	693	50	496	192	192	19

Experiment Details. We use the pre-trained T5-large [9] model as a sequence-to-sequence model with a word embedding dimension of 1024. In the training stage, the learning rate is $2e-4$ and the training batch size is 16. The number of training epochs is 20 for all experiments. During the inference, we utilize greedy decoding for generating the output sequence.

Baselines. We compare our method with five baselines.

- **RoBERTa**: The method uses RoBERTa [6] as an encoder to extract sentiment elements using a span-based recognition method. For each sentiment expression, all sentiment targets in the sentence are selected as sentiment targets for their corresponding sentiment structure and all sentiment holders in the sentence as sentiment holders for their corresponding sentiment structure.
- **Pipeline**: The method first uses RoBERTa [6] as an encoder to extract sentiment elements using a span-based recognition method. For each sentiment expression, the relatively closest sentiment target is selected as the sentiment target of its corresponding sentiment structure and the closest sentiment holder as the sentiment holder of its corresponding sentiment structure.
- **GTS** [13]: The method uses a grid annotation to simultaneously annotate segments and relationships between segments, in this way the method transforms SSA into a sequence annotation task.

- **head-first** [3]: The method translates fragment extraction and relationship prediction into a prediction of the relationship between each word in a similar syntactic structure tree, where spans that are related are linked by their first word.
- **head-final** [3]: The method translates fragment extraction and relationship prediction into a prediction of the relationship between each word in a similar syntactic structure tree, where spans that are related are linked by their final word.

Table 6. Main results of the SSA task. The best results are in bold.

Model	OpeNER			MPQA			DS_unis		
	P	R	$SF1$	P	R	$SF1$	P	R	$SF1$
GTS	33.18	40.42	36.45	10.10	12.51	11.18	30.81	22.35	25.91
head-first	58.37	41.89	48.77	29.53	12.75	17.81	**44.34**	23.95	31.10
head-final	40.92	40.26	40.59	24.51	18.21	20.90	28.55	20.13	23.61
RoBERTa	32.91	57.21	41.79	32.73	33.06	32.89	36.17	29.51	32.50
Pipeline	57.53	53.30	55.33	38.79	32.21	35.19	34.99	26.27	30.01
seq2seq-N	**71.97**	67.07	69.44	37.46	31.59	34.27	31.20	27.46	29.21
seq2seq-T	71.07	**72.94**	**71.99**	**43.30**	**35.24**	**38.85**	39.32	**30.29**	**34.22**

4   Results and Discussions

4.1   Main Results

The result for the SSA task is reported in Table 6. For the model that uses natural language templates to generate target sequences, it is named seq2seq-N. For the model that uses tuple sequence template to generate target sequences, it is named seq2seq-T. There are some notable observations: the seq2seq-T model outperforms all comparative models on all three datasets and the seq2seq-N model OpeNER outperforms all comparative models on the OpeNER dataset. This demonstrates the effectiveness of the our method in SSA. Compared to the seq2seq-N model, the performance of seq2seq-T was improved on all datasets. This suggests that the model using tuple sequence templates is more suitable for the SSA task, where the possible reason is that the natural language template based approach cannot filter some of the implausible generated sequences in the decoding stage.

Table 7. Ablation study for contribution of label semantics.

Model	OpeNER			MPQA			DS_unis		
	P	R	$SF1$	P	R	$SF1$	P	R	$SF1$
seq2seq-N w/o p	71.63	67.22	69.35	37.58	31.43	34.23	31.42	27.33	29.23
seq2seq-T w/o p	69.58	70.82	70.19	40.92	**35.27**	37.89	**39.82**	29.87	34.13
seq2seq-N	**71.97**	67.07	69.44	37.46	31.59	34.27	31.20	27.46	29.21
seq2seq-T	71.07	**72.94**	**71.99**	**43.30**	35.24	**38.85**	39.32	**30.29**	**34.22**

Effect of Label Semantics. To verify that the proposed approach can effectively exploit the semantic knowledge in the labels, ablation experiments are designed to further analyse the impact of label semantics on model performance. For polarity labels, the comparison method maps them into a series of special symbols. Specifically, positive is mapped as P1; negative is mapped as P2; and neutral is mapped as P3. The results of the experiments are shown in Table 7, where seq2seq-N w/o p indicates that the seq2seq-N uses special symbol labels; seq2seq-T w/o p indicates that seq2seq-T uses special symbol labels. From the experimental results, it can be observed that the performance of the model decreases in most datasets when the semantic information from sentiment polarity labels is not utilized. This supports the motivation behind using the sequence-to-sequence model in this work: compared to the sequence annotation model that treats emotion polarity labels as meaningless tags, the sequence-to-sequence model, by designing appropriate templates, can better leverage the semantic information within the labels. Furthermore, it can be observed that for some of the datasets, the performance of the model does not degrade significantly when the semantic information in the sentiment polarity labels is removed. The possible reason for this is that there are only three types of sentiment polarity in the datasets, and therefore the model learns the mapping between special symbols and sentiment polarity types during training easily.

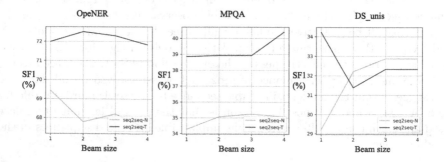

Fig. 2. The results for different beam size.

Effect of Beam Search. In order to assess the effect of beam size on the performance of the generative model in beam search, we use different beam sizes and observes the corresponding model performance. The experimental results are shown in Fig. 2. As can be seen from the figure, there is no clear tendency for the beam size to affect the performance of the models. Also the larger the beam size, the larger the search space and the corresponding increase in the time complexity of the model, so the appropriate beam size should be chosen according to the actual situation.

5 Conclusion

In this paper, we address the SSA task by transforming it into a sequence generation task and propose a generative model for SSA. To leverage the semantic information encoded in the labels, we design two templates for constructing the target sequence. Additionally, in the decoding stage, we employ a series of rules to enhance the accuracy of sentiment structure prediction. Through experiments conducted on SSA datasets, we demonstrate the effectiveness of our proposed model.

Acknowledgement. This research was supported in part by the National Natural Science Foundation of China (62006062, 62176076), Natural Science Foundation of Guangdong (2023A1515012922), and Key Technologies Research and Development Program of Shenzhen JSGG20210802154400001.

References

1. Agerri, R., Cuadros, M., Gaines, S., Rigau, G.: OpeNER: open polarity enhanced named entity recognition. In: Sociedad Española para el Procesamiento del Lenguaje Natural, vol. 51, pp. 215–218 (2013)
2. Athiwaratkun, B., dos Santos, C., Krone, J., Xiang, B.: Augmented natural language for generative sequence labeling. In: Proceedings of the 2020 Conference on Empirical Methods in Natural Language Processing (EMNLP), pp. 375–385 (2020)
3. Barnes, J., Kurtz, R., Oepen, S., Øvrelid, L., Velldal, E.: Structured sentiment analysis as dependency graph parsing. In: Proceedings of the 59th Annual Meeting of the Association for Computational Linguistics and the 11th International Joint Conference on Natural Language Processing (Volume 1: Long Papers), pp. 3387–3402 (2021)
4. Katiyar, A., Cardie, C.: Investigating LSTMS for joint extraction of opinion entities and relations. In: Proceedings of the 54th Annual Meeting of the Association for Computational Linguistics (Volume 1: Long Papers), pp. 919–929 (2016)
5. Liu, X., et al.: GPT understands, too. arXiv preprint arXiv:2103.10385 (2021)
6. Liu, Y., et al.: Roberta: a robustly optimized bert pretraining approach. arXiv preprint arXiv:1907.11692 (2019)
7. Paolini, G., et al.: Structured prediction as translation between augmented natural languages. In: International Conference on Learning Representations (2020)
8. Peng, L., Li, Z., Zhao, H.: Sparse fuzzy attention for structured sentiment analysis. arXiv preprint arXiv:2109.06719 (2021)

9. Raffel, C., et al.: Exploring the limits of transfer learning with a unified text-to-text transformer. J. Mach. Learn. Res. **21**(1), 5485–5551 (2020)
10. Toprak, C., Jakob, N., Gurevych, I.: Sentence and expression level annotation of opinions in user-generated discourse. In: Proceedings of the 48th Annual Meeting of the Association for Computational Linguistics, pp. 575–584 (2010)
11. Vaswani, A., et al.: Attention is all you need. In: Advances in Neural Information Processing Systems, vol. 30 (2017)
12. Wiebe, J., Wilson, T., Cardie, C.: Annotating expressions of opinions and emotions in language. Lang. Resour. Eval. **39**(2–3), 165–210 (2005)
13. Wu, Z., Ying, C., Zhao, F., Fan, Z., Dai, X., Xia, R.: Grid tagging scheme for aspect-oriented fine-grained opinion extraction. In: Findings of the Association for Computational Linguistics, EMNLP 2020, pp. 2576–2585 (2020)
14. Xia, Q., et al.: A unified span-based approach for opinion mining with syntactic constituents. In: Proceedings of the 2021 Conference of the North American Chapter of the Association for Computational Linguistics: Human Language Technologies, pp. 1795–1804 (2021)
15. Xu, Q., Li, B., Li, F., Fu, G., Ji, D.: A dual-pointer guided transition system for end-to-end structured sentiment analysis with global graph reasoning. Inf. Process. Manage. **59**(4), 102992 (2022)
16. Zhang, W., Deng, Y., Li, X., Yuan, Y., Bing, L., Lam, W.: Aspect sentiment quad prediction as paraphrase generation. In: Proceedings of the 2021 Conference on Empirical Methods in Natural Language Processing, pp. 9209–9219 (2021)

Artificial Bee Colony Algorithm Based on Quantum Bloch Spherical Optimization

Na Sun[iD], Zeyu Ren[✉][iD], and Xuwen Liao[iD]

Minzu University of China, Beijing 10081, China
rzy0220@163.com

Abstract. The swarm intelligence optimization algorithm has strong adaptability to optimization problems, fast computational speed, and the ability to quickly find the optimal solution, demonstrating a momentum of rapid development. As a type of swarm intelligence optimization algorithm, artificial bee colony algorithm obtains the optimal solution through the cyclic foraging and iteration of hired bees, observation bees, and reconnaissance bees, and has now been widely applied in various fields, But the artificial bee colony algorithm has the shortcomings of slow Rate of convergence and easy to fall into the local optimal solution. To overcome these shortcomings, this paper proposes an artificial bee colony algorithm based on the quantum Bloch spherical optimization mechanism. The effectiveness of the algorithm is proved through six benchmark test functions. The experimental results of the convergence curve graph can show that the Rate of convergence is greatly accelerated, and the global optimal solution can be obtained quickly.

Keywords: artificial bee colony · Swarm intelligence optimization algorithm · Quantum Optimization Bloch Spherical Optimization Mechanism

1 Introduction

1.1 Research Significance of Artificial Bee Colony Algorithm

Optimization problems are commonly encountered in fields such as national defense, scientific engineering, management, economics, finance, transportation, and computer science. They typically involve selecting the optimal solution from various feasible solutions and constructing computational methods to seek the optimal solution. The idea of bionic optimization algorithm is derived from the evolution and adaptive phenomenon of Biological system. It does not rely on strict mathematical relations, but simulates the social or survival behavior of organisms in nature, so its application scope is wider than traditional algorithms. From the perspective of practical applications, intelligent optimization algorithms do not require analytical properties such as continuity, differentiability, and differentiability of the objective function, or even function expressions, nor do they require the selection of initial points for the algorithm. They have strong adaptability to specific optimization problems, and their calculation speed is very fast, enabling them to quickly find the optimal solution to the problem, These advantages have

Y. Yang et al. (Eds.): AIMS 2023, LNCS 14202, pp. 39–49, 2023.
https://doi.org/10.1007/978-3-031-45140-9_4

attracted widespread attention from many scholars since the birth of intelligent optimization algorithms, and they will inevitably receive deeper research and wider applications in the future. Because of its simple algorithm, easy implementation, and fast Rate of convergence, the artificial bee colony algorithm has attracted extensive attention from many scholars. It generates the optimal solution through the cooperation mechanism of the population, which is different from the genetic algorithm that generates the optimal solution through the competition mechanism of the population. The artificial bee colony algorithm has been widely used in function optimization problems, artificial neural network training, UAV path selection and other problems, Similar to other intelligent optimization technologies, the artificial bee colony algorithm has the disadvantages of slow Rate of convergence and easy to fall into local optimum. The main reason is that the search mode of the algorithm has good exploration ability, but weak development ability.

1.2 Research Status of Artificial Bee Colony Algorithm

The artificial bee colony algorithm is a heuristic optimization algorithm originally developed by Dervi ş Karabo ğ A proposed in 2005 to simulate the behavior of bees in exploring and selecting food.X. Bing, Z. Youwei, Z. Xueyan and S. Xuekai proposed an improved artificial bee colony algorithm for the shortcomings of fast early convergence and easy to fall into local optimum. The IABC algorithm was tested with standard test functions Ackley, Griewink, Schaffer and Sphere. The results show that the algorithm not only accelerates the Rate of convergence, but also improves the optimal value found, providing better optimization performance. Lingling Zhang proposed a new gravity artificial bee colony (GABC) optimization algorithm and applied it to unsupervised pattern recognition problems. GABC has high precision and Rate of convergence. Then, the performance of the GABC based clustering model was tested using test data and fault samples, demonstrating its superiority in effectiveness and efficiency. H. Li, Y. Zhang, Z. Dan, L. Ma, C. Zhang and Q. Wang proposed the Tabu search artificial bee colony algorithm. In the interference countermeasure scenario, the algorithm proposed in this article was compared with the ABC algorithm and PSO algorithm. The simulation results show that the proposed TSABC algorithm effectively improves the interference efficiency and can quickly and accurately interfere with a large number of unmanned aerial vehicles. H. Aoyang, Z. Shengqi, J. Xuehui and Z. Zhisheng established an RBF neural network short-term load forecasting model based on artificial bee colony algorithm optimization, because the artificial bee colony algorithm has the advantages of simple implementation, strong global search ability, and strong robustness. It can quickly jump out of local optima, verifying that the RBF neural network model optimized based on artificial bee colony algorithm can achieve satisfactory prediction results. Andr é s Arostegui; Diego S. Ben í tez; Luis Caiza proposed a fuzzy PD controller design based on artificial bee colony optimization algorithm based on the intelligent foraging behavior of bee colonies. Then, the proposed optimization controller is applied to the temperature control of the heat exchanger in large-scale pasteurization equipment. C. In order to improve the accuracy of the Artificial Bee Colony Algorithm (ABC) in Vehicle Routing Problem with Time Windows (VRPTW), Chen and K. Zhou changed the single search mode to a ternary search method, which improved the optimization depth of the algorithm.

Multiple neighborhood searches were conducted for food sources, and the next iteration was conducted to improve the survival rate of new food sources and increase population diversity. Record global optimal solutions by setting and updating bulletin boards. Simulation experiments have shown that the improved discrete ABC algorithm has significant advantages in solving large-scale VRPTW problems. A. Lefteh, M. Houshmand, M. Khorrampanah, and G. F. Smaisim used an improved adaptive neurofuzzy inference system (MANFIS) and artificial bee colony algorithm to classify benign and malignant bone cancer. The experiment shows that the proposed method has a high accuracy of 96.67% in bone MR images.

1.3   The Application of Artificial Bee Colony Algorithm

In recent years, the ABC algorithm has been widely applied in various fields. In China, the ABC algorithm has also been increasingly applied in optimization problems, such as achieving good results in power systems, control systems, engineering design, and other aspects. At the same time, researchers have also made many improvements and optimizations to this algorithm, such as the maximum power tracking control of photovoltaic power generation based on the improved ABC algorithm, and the combination of ABC algorithm and artificial neural network. In foreign countries, the ABC algorithm has also been widely applied and studied. For example, in the field of data mining, the ABC algorithm is used for clustering and classification tasks. In addition, ABC algorithm is also used to optimize flight mission track, Feature selection in machine learning and other fields.

Artificial bee colony algorithm is a heuristic optimization algorithm that can achieve good results in practical applications. The following are some specific application areas: deployment issues in wireless sensor networks: using ABC algorithm to optimize the deployment of sensors in wireless sensor networks to achieve optimal coverage, communication quality, and energy savings. Feature selection in machine learning: ABC algorithm can be used for Feature selection. In a dataset containing a large number of variables, select the most important features to improve the accuracy of classification and regression. Photovoltaic power generation maximum power tracking control: The improved ABC algorithm is used for maximum power tracking control of photovoltaic power generation systems, which enables the photovoltaic power generation system to respond quickly and maintain maximum output power in the event of changes in light intensity.

Multi objective optimization problems: The ABC algorithm can be applied to multi-objective optimization problems, such as network routing problems and economic scheduling problems. Power system scheduling: The ABC algorithm can be used to optimize the economic scheduling of the power system, reduce energy waste, and improve power generation efficiency. Object detection and tracking in machine vision: Use ABC algorithm to optimize object detection and tracking algorithms to improve computational efficiency and accuracy. In summary, the application and research of the ABC algorithm at home and abroad have gradually gained widespread attention and recognition, and more scholars and industry applications will explore its potential in the future.

2 Artificial Bee Colony

2.1 Introduction to Artificial Bee Colony Algorithm

In the initialization phase, initialize the parameters of the ABC algorithm, which include the number of honey sources SN, the limit of the number of times the honey source is discarded, and the number of iteration terminations. In the standard ABC algorithm, the number of honey sources SN is equal to the number of hired bees and also equal to the number of following bees. The formula for generating a certain honey source is:

$$x_{ij} = x_j^{min} + rand(0, 1)\left(x_j^{max} - x_j^{min}\right)$$

where $i = 1,2,\ldots,$ SN, $j = 1,2,\ldots,$ D, SN are the number of food sources, D is the number of design parameters (i.e. dimensions), and are the lower and upper bounds of the jth dimension, respectively.

The initial population was improved through the foraging cycle of hiring bees, observing bees, and reconnaissance bees, and the foraging cycle will continue to iterate until the termination criteria are met. The termination criterion can be to reach the maximum number of evaluations or to find an acceptable function value.

In the stage of hiring bees, local searches are conducted within the field of food sources to simulate food source extraction in real foraging behavior. The local search of the basic ABC algorithm is defined by Eq. (2):

$$v_{ij} = x_{ij} + \phi_{ij}\left(x_{ij} - x_{kj}\right)$$

where i is the current solution, k is the randomly selected neighborhood solution, and is a random number that follows a uniform distribution between [-1,1]. In the local search defined in the above formula, only one randomly selected dimension (parameter j) in the current solution has been changed. After the local search is completed, greedily choose the better solution between the current solution and the mutated solution to preserve and discard the worse solution. Each food source in the population applies local search and greedy selection.

Once the hiring bee phase is completed, start observing the beginning of the bee phase. At this stage, the neighborhood of the food source will be searched to find a better solution similar to that in the hiring bee stage. The difference is that the search is not performed one by one near each solution. On the contrary, the solutions to be searched are randomly selected based on fitness values, which means high-quality solutions are more likely to be selected, which is the positive feedback attribute of the ABC algorithm. The probability of selecting each solution is proportional to its fitness value:

$$p_i = \frac{\text{fitness}_i}{\sum_{i=1}^{SN} \text{fitness}_i}$$

After calculating the probability value, a fitness based selection mechanism is used to have a greater chance of selecting the optimal solution. The selection mechanisms can be roulette, ranking based, random traversal sampling, tournaments, etc. In the basic ABC, roulette is used, which is similar to real bee colonies. Based on the dance information of hired bees, a better food source will attract more bees' attention. Once SN solutions are selected with probability, local searches are performed near these solutions, followed by greedy searches to obtain better solutions. During the stages of hiring bees and observing bees, if local search fails to improve the solution, the counter is increased by 1, which stores the number of times this solution has been utilized and retained in the population. Therefore, this is similar to the number of food sources developed by bees in reality. In reality, as simulated in the ABC algorithm, the nectar of a food source is depleted at the end of mining. If a food source is fully exploited, it will be abandoned by its bees. A counter is used to determine the adequacy and depletion of mining. If the counter exceeds the limit, the solution associated with the counter is considered exhausted and then replaced by a new solution randomly generated by Eq. (1).

Artificial bee colony algorithm process:

Algorithm: Artificial Bee Colony Algorithm.

Provide initial population using random initialization method, evaluate population quality, and initialize algorithm parameters.

Step 1. Initialize algorithm parameters to generate the initial position of bees.

Step 2. Hire bees to calculate fitness values, compare and save the optimal values.

Step 3. Follow the bee to select the hired bee to update the honey source location, calculate the fitness value, and save the best value.

Step 4. If a reconnaissance bee appears, regenerate the initial position and perform update optimization. Otherwise, continue with Step 5.

Step 5. If the number of iterations is less than the preset number of iterations, go to step 2; Otherwise, output the optimal solution.

3   Quantum Bloch Optimization Mechanism

3.1   Introduction to Quantum Bloch Optimization Mechanism

Quantum Evolutionary algorithm is a new optimization algorithm based on quantum computing, which is often used to solve complex Combinatorial optimization problems. In order to improve the slow convergence speed and easy falling into local optima of artificial bee colony algorithm in solving multivariable optimization problems, a new quantum optimization algorithm is proposed by combining quantum theory and artificial bee colony algorithm. The algorithm uses quantized Bloch coordinates to encode the food source in the bee colony algorithm, expanding the number of global optimal solutions and increasing the probability of the bee colony algorithm obtaining the global optimal solution. In experiments on typical function optimization problems, the proposed algorithm outperforms the artificial bee colony algorithm in terms of search ability and optimization efficiency. Quantum Bloch sphere optimization mechanism is one of the optimization strategies, which is used to find the global optimal solution in the quantum space. Its specific idea is to use the Bloch sphere in quantum computing to describe the evolution process of Quantum state, so as to achieve global optimization.

In quantum computing, the state of a system can be represented by a linear combination of multiple ground states, and can be represented by a vector on a Bloch sphere. Specifically, a vector starting from the center of a sphere and passing through a point on the sphere can be represented by the longitude and latitude on the sphere. The quantum algorithm can rotate and flip this vector according to specific rules, and get the final result through Measurement in quantum mechanics.

The optimization mechanism of quantum Bloch sphere is based on this process of Quantum state evolution to achieve optimization. The specific steps are as follows: convert each optimization parameter (such as vector) into a corresponding Quantum state, and use Bloch sphere to represent it; According to the rules of quantum algorithm, each Quantum state is rotated and flipped to gradually evolve into a Quantum state near the global optimal solution; According to the results of Measurement in quantum mechanics, the final optimization parameters, namely the global optimal solution, are obtained.

By using the Bloch sphere evolution process in quantum computing, the quantum Bloch sphere optimization mechanism of quantum Evolutionary algorithm can efficiently search the global optimal solution in quantum space. However, this algorithm still has some limitations, such as requiring a large amount of computing resources and complex quantum algorithm support.

Study the optimization mechanism of quantum Bloch sphere. The quantum Evolutionary algorithm is used to study the transformation relationship between the qubit and the solution vector, establish the transformation model of the feasible solution space and the fitness function, thus expanding the number of global optimal solutions, which can greatly improve the probability of global optimal solutions and overcome the premature phenomenon.

The quantum Bloch spherical optimization mechanism is an optimization strategy used in quantum computing to solve optimization problems. This mechanism is based on the motion of quantum bits on Bloch balls for searching, thereby achieving optimization of optimization problems.

Specifically, when performing optimization, this mechanism first transforms the problem to be solved into a problem that can construct a Hamiltonian. Then encode the Hamiltonian onto the quantum bit, enabling it to evolve. During the evolution process, quantum bits will move along a certain path on the Bloch sphere, thereby achieving problem optimization.

In this process, the state of each quantum bit can be represented as a point in the Bloch sphere. During the evolution of quantum bits along different paths on a sphere, their motion on the Bloch sphere can be represented as a line segment or arc length on the Bloch sphere. This path is the most optimal solution to the problem to be solved.

In practical applications, the quantum Bloch spherical optimization mechanism can be used to solve various optimization problems, such as graph coloring, routing, and so on. Compared with classical algorithms, this mechanism can find better solutions in a shorter time, so it has good application prospects.

Combining the artificial bee colony algorithm (ABC) and quantum Evolutionary algorithm (QEA), we can use the advantages of the two algorithms to improve the optimization effect. Among them, the quantum Bloch spherical optimization mechanism can be used to search for global optimal solutions in quantum space, while the ABC algorithm can be used to search for local optimal solutions in classical space and achieve fast convergence of optimization speed.

Specifically, the specific algorithm is as follows:

Algorithm: Artificial Bee Colony Algorithm Based on Quantum Bloch Spherical Optimization.

Step 1: Use the ABC algorithm to initialize the population, optimize it in classical space, and record the current optimal solution.

Step 2: Convert the current optimal solution to a Quantum state, and use the quantum Bloch spherical optimization mechanism to optimize in quantum space.

Step 3: Convert the optimal solution obtained from quantum space back to classical space and compare it with the optimal solution obtained from ABC algorithm, selecting the better solution as the next round of population initialization.

Step 4: Loop through steps 2–3 until the stop iteration condition is met.

By combining the two algorithms, the optimal solution can be found in classical and quantum spaces based on the different characteristics of the optimization problem, thereby improving the optimization effect. Meanwhile, in practical applications, it is necessary to adjust the algorithm parameters and optimization process according to specific problems to achieve better results.

4 Numerical Experiment

In this paper, the optimisation performance of the improved artificial bee colony algorithm is verified using six benchmark test functions selected as shown in Table 2, all of which have dimension D = 30 and a population size of 50.The maximum, minimum, and mean values are the maximum, minimum, and mean values of the optimal solutions for each test function after running the ABC algorithm and QABC algorithm 30 times, respectively (Table 1 and Figs. 1, 2, 3, 4, 5 and 6).

Table 1. Basic Table of Test Functions.

function name	function expression	Possible solution space
sphere	$f = \sum_{i=1}^{n} x_i^2$	$[-100,100]$
rosenbrock	$f = \sum_{i=1}^{n-1}\left[100\left(x_{i+1} - x_i^2\right)^2 + (x_i - 1)^2\right]$	$[-30,30]$
ackley	$f = -20\exp\left(-0.2\sqrt{\frac{1}{n}\sum_{i=1}^{n}x_i^2}\right) -$ $\exp\left(\frac{1}{n}\sum_{i=1}^{n}\cos(2\pi x_i)\right) + 2$	$[-32,32]$
rastrigin	$f = \sum_{i=1}^{n}\left[x_i^2 - 10\cos(2\pi x_i) + 10\right]$	$[-5.12,5.12]$
griewank	$f = \frac{1}{4000}\sum_{i=1}^{n}x_i^2 - \prod_{i=1}^{n}\cos\left(\frac{x_i}{\sqrt{i}}\right) + 1$	$[-600,600]$
schwefel	$f = \sum_{i=1}^{n} - x_i\sin\left(\sqrt{|x_i|}\right)$	$[-500,500]$

Table 2. Comparison Table of Test Results.

function name	algorithm	Mean	Best	Worst
sphere	ABC	990.880759004292	0.005239022782134984	3198.3364642564243
	QABC	0.07733044739583281	0.007839884563195445	0.3936540369380858
rosenbrock	ABC	212.9244189105304	26.736172368784434	1815.7335231303393
	QABC	63.3800288502284	7.347878131230892	125.36861390619563
ackley	ABC	18.987461536899595	18.59918721726783	19.36679617559856
	QABC	0.2726170788979399	0.14317375328697368	0.9786477077892042
rastrigin	ABC	140.88632484936943	109.39602276186841	183.0978229047019
	QABC	28.260160967419214	5.531470841130661	46.97397077640797
griewank	ABC	2.2590683088689776	0.3437042619185997	5.685058211963045
	QABC	0.003672421584964691	0.000713980227247113	0.012573455106566267
schwefel	ABC	−5746.088747454827	−3591.691677101014	−9794.3343263609
	QABC	−4298.761784730316	−3660.8502203369494	−4994.257648556701

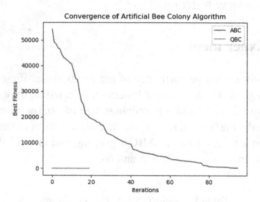

Fig. 1. Comparison of convergence performance between QABC and ABC in sphere function

Through the comparison of experimental results, it was found that the average of the optimal values obtained by the improved artificial bee colony algorithm based on quantum Bloch sphere is equal to or close to the optimal value of the test function. Among them, for single mode functions, the results obtained by the improved artificial bee colony algorithm are closer to the optimal value than the artificial bee colony algorithm; For multimodal functions, improving the artificial bee colony algorithm can obtain the optimal value of the problem, while the artificial bee colony algorithm cannot obtain the optimal value under the same experimental conditions. Moreover, when the dimension of the test problem increases, the hybrid artificial bee colony algorithm can obtain more stable experimental results. These results all indicate that improving the artificial bee colony algorithm can obtain the optimal solution or a solution closer to the optimal solution of the test function, and the stability of the algorithm is better.

Artificial bee colony algorithm is a new type of swarm intelligence optimization technology that demonstrates good optimization performance. However, this algorithm,

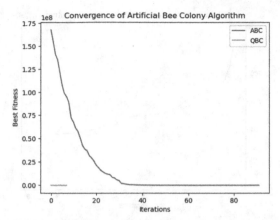

Fig. 2. Comparison of convergence performance between QABC and ABC in Rosenbrock function

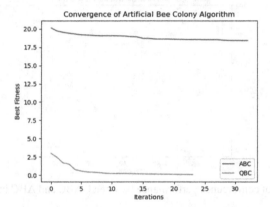

Fig. 3. Comparison of convergence performance between QABC and ABC in Ackley function

like other intelligent optimization technologies, has the disadvantages of slow Rate of convergence and easy to fall into local optimum. The main reason is that the search mode of this algorithm has good exploration ability, but weak development ability. In order to overcome these shortcomings, this paper proposes an improved artificial bee colony algorithm based on the quantum BLOCH spherical optimization mechanism. The test and comparative study of the test function show that the improved artificial bee colony algorithm proposed in this chapter is superior to the artificial bee colony algorithm in accuracy, Rate of convergence, stability and robustness, Compared with other intelligent optimization algorithms, the improved artificial bee colony algorithm proposed in this chapter has better optimization performance and stability.

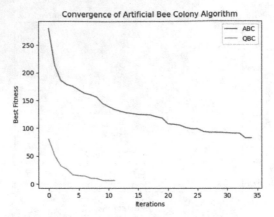

Fig. 4. Comparison of convergence performance between QABC and ABC in rastrigin function

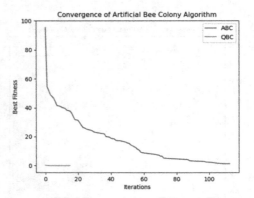

Fig. 5. Comparison of convergence performance between QABC and ABC in griewank function

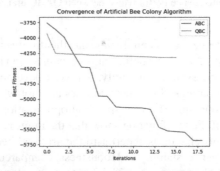

Fig. 6. Comparison of convergence performance between QABC and ABC in Schwefel function

References

1. Aoyang, H., Shengqi, Z., Xuehui, J., Zhisheng, Z.: Short-term load forecasting model based on RBF neural network optimized by artificial bee colony algorithm. In: 2021 IEEE 2nd

International Conference on Big Data, Artificial Intelligence and Internet of Things Engineering (ICBAIE), Nanchang, China, pp. 486–489 (2021)
2. Zhang, L.: A gravitational artificial bee colony optimization algorithm and application. In: 2018 Eighth International Conference on Instrumentation & Measurement, Computer, Communication and Control (IMCCC), Harbin, China, pp. 1839–1842 (2018)
3. Li, H., Zhang, Y., Dan, Z., Ma, L., Zhang, C., Wang, Q.: Distributed interference optimization method of large-scale UAV based on tabu search artificial bee colony algorithm. In: 2022 IEEE International Conference on Signal Processing, Communications and Computing (ICSPCC), Xi'an, China, pp. 1–5 (2022)
4. Arostegui, A., Benítez, D.S., Caiza, L.: A fuzzy-PD controller optimized by artificial bee colony algorithm applied to a small-scale pasteurization plant. In: 2020 IEEE ANDESCON, Quito, Ecuador, pp. 1–6 (2020)
5. Bing, X., Youwei, Z., Xueyan, Z., Xuekai, S.: An improved artificial bee colony algorithm based on faster convergence. In: 2021 IEEE International Conference on Artificial Intelligence and Computer Applications (ICAICA), Dalian, China, pp. 776–779 (2021). https://doi.org/10.1109/ICAICA52286.2021.9498254
6. Chen, C., Zhou, K.: Application of artificial bee colony algorithm in vehicle routing problem with time windows. In: 2018 International Conference on Sensing, Diagnostics, Prognostics, and Control (SDPC), Xi'an, China, pp. 781–785 (2018). https://doi.org/10.1109/SDPC.2018.8664999
7. Lefteh, A., Houshmand, M., Khorrampanah, M., Smaisim, G.F.: Optimization of modified adaptive neuro-fuzzy inference system (MANFIS) with artificial bee colony (ABC) algorithm for classification of bone cancer. In: 2022 Second International Conference on Distributed Computing and High Performance Computing (DCHPC), Qom, Iran, Islamic Republic of, pp. 78–81 (2022). https://doi.org/10.1109/DCHPC55044.2022.9731840
8. Pian, J., Abdulmajid, A.U., Tamanna, M., Sun, L.: Improved bee colony algorithm and its application in optimization of thermal expansion coefficient. In: 2022 34th Chinese Control and Decision Conference (CCDC), Hefei, China, pp. 262-267 (2022). https://doi.org/10.1109/CCDC55256.2022.10033645

Traffic Flow Prediction Based on Attention Mechanism Convolutional Neural Network

Sumin Li, Jing Li, Jie Lan, and Yong Lu[✉]

School of Information Engineering, Minzu University of China, Beijing 100081, China
{smli,21302002,20011437,2006153}@muc.edu.cn

Abstract. Traffic flow prediction is one of the core issues in the field of transportation planning and management. Traditional traffic flow prediction methods are limited by factors such as data sparsity, long-term interdependencies, and intricate spatiotemporal dynamics. To overcome these challenges, this paper proposes a novel predictive model called ARSTGCN, which incorporates spatiotemporal attention mechanisms and deep learning networks. Firstly, the spatiotemporal attention mechanism assigns attention weights to traffic sensor nodes, enabling the capture of spatiotemporal relationships. Dilation convolution is employed to process the temporal correlation in the data, mitigating concerns of gradient explosion and vanishing during the training of lengthy time series. Secondly, data containing spatiotemporal weight features undergoes input into the graph convolutional network, facilitating the capture of spatial dynamic correlations. The final prediction results are obtained through the utilization of the fully connected layer. Compared with the baseline model on two publicly available datasets, ARSTGCN showed certain advantages.

Keywords: Traffic Flow Prediction · Attention Mechanism · Graph Convolution

1 Introduction

With the continuous development of China's transportation industry and the sharp increase in vehicles, traffic congestion and frequent traffic accidents have emerged as critical challenges confronted by modern cities. To overcome these issues, experts have shifted their focus towards establishing an intelligent transportation system (ITS) [1]. The objective is to develop smart transportation and transportation information technology, enhance the efficiency and precision of traffic control, while optimizing traffic flow, with the ultimate aim of alleviating the prevailing traffic problems.

So far, research on traffic flow prediction has a history of over a decade. Initially, mathematical and physical methods were commonly employed for prediction. The most typical models included the Historical Average (HA) model [2], Vector Autoregressive (VAR) model [3], and Autoregressive Integrated Moving Average (ARIMA) model [4]. However, these models relied on linear data analysis, while traffic flow data is nonlinear and complex. Therefore, statistical-based prediction methods did not adequately fit traffic flow data. Some common machine learning methods used in the field of traffic

Y. Yang et al. (Eds.): AIMS 2023, LNCS 14202, pp. 50–59, 2023.
https://doi.org/10.1007/978-3-031-45140-9_5

flow prediction include Support Vector Machine (SVM), K-Nearest Neighbors (KNN) algorithm, and Kalman filter model [5]. In the 1990s, SVM proposed by Vapnik et al. in the literature [6] has gained considerable attention. SVM is a supervised learning algorithm that separates samples into two categories by defining an optimal boundary. It was employed in traffic flow prediction to overcome the limitations of traditional statistical models in handling nonlinear problems. In literature [7], Zhang et al. proposed a short-term traffic flow prediction method based on Balanced Binary Tree K-Nearest Neighbor Non-parametric Regression. This method utilized clustering and a balanced binary tree structure to establish a case database, aiming to improve prediction accuracy and meet real-time requirements. These machine learning methods offered new avenues for enhancing the accuracy and reliability of traffic flow prediction. However, machine learning models needed to possess good generalization ability when predicting new traffic flow data. Yet, due to the complexity and dynamic nature of the traffic system, the generalization ability of the models was limited across different regions, time periods, or traffic scenarios.

In recent years, with the emergence of deep learning models, researchers have gradually employed deep neural network models for traffic flow prediction. Ma et al. [8] utilized Long Short-Term Memory (LSTM) neural networks for predicting traffic speeds, effectively capturing the temporal correlations in the data flow. Literature [9] combines the convolutional neural network (CNN) and LSTM to extract the spatiotemporal features from multiple perspectives, and the experimental results show that this method can effectively predict traffic information. Although these models have made significant progress in feature extraction, they still cannot represent the true non-Euclidean spatial road network structure [10]. Some scholars have studied the graph convolutional network (GCN). Li et al. [11] proposed the DCRNN model, combining the characteristics of diffusion graph convolution and recurrent neural network to capture the spatiotemporal dependence in traffic data. Yu et al. [12] designed the STGCN model using spatial graph convolution and temporal convolution to effectively model the spatiotemporal dependencies in traffic data and improve traffic prediction accuracy. Subsequently, Guo et al. [13] introduced the ASTGCN model by adding attention mechanisms to the STGCN model. Geng et al. [14] proposed the SMGCN model for predicting the demand of ride-hailing services. This model combines spatiotemporal features and multi-graph convolution operations, aiming to capture the spatiotemporal dependencies in the data related to ride-hailing service demand.

Although existing deep learning methods consider the temporal and spatial correlations, these methods still have shortcomings. Most of these methods rely on LSTM and GRU to capture temporal dependencies, which can easily lead to the problems of gradient explosion and vanishing when dealing with long time series. Additionally, some network models attempt to use stacked one-dimensional convolutions to mitigate the gradient explosion issue, leading to an increase in computational complexity.

To overcome these limitations, fully consider the spatiotemporal dynamic correlation, and further improve the accuracy of traffic flow prediction, this paper reduces the model complexity and improves the operating efficiency by reducing the number of network layers on the basis of the ASTGCN model. In addition, the dilated convolution is introduced based on the existing baseline model to extract long-time dynamic correlations with fewer network layers and parameters to improve the prediction accuracy. Therefore, this paper proposes a new traffic flow prediction method called ARSTGCN.

2 ARSTGCN Model

2.1 Problem Definition

Traffic flow prediction refers to the use of traffic flow data collected by traffic sensors distributed on the road [15] to predict the future traffic flow of a certain location or area. That is, the number of vehicles passing through the location or area in a certain period of time in the future.

Definition 1 (Traffic Road Network G). The sensors in the road network constitute a topology diagram $G = (V, E, A)$, where V is the set of nodes, indicating the sensor nodes in the road network, the number of nodes is N, $V = \{v_1, v_2, v_3, \ldots v_n\}$; E is the set of edges, indicating the connectivity between the sensors; $A \in R^{N \times N}$ is the adjacency matrix constructed based on the distances between sensors, representing the connectivity between nodes.

Definition 2 (Graph Signal Matrix X). The traffic flow observed on graph G is represented as the graph signal $X \in R^{N \times P}$, where P represents the number of features of each node. The traffic flow prediction problem involves learning a mapping function $f(\cdot)$ for the traffic flow at a given graph G and historical T time period to predict future traffic information for T'. The mapping relationship is shown in Eq. (1).

$$(X_{t+1}, X_{t+2}, \cdots, X_{t+T'} = f(G; (X_{t-T+1}, \cdots, X_{t-1}, X_t)) \tag{1}$$

2.2 Model Framework

The overall framework of this paper is illustrated in Fig. 1, which consists of a residual layer, a spatiotemporal convolutional block, and a fully connected layer. The spatiotemporal convolutional block is composed of two temporal convolutions (TCM) and one graph convolution (GCN), and incorporates spatiotemporal attention mechanisms to extract features from both the temporal and spatial dimensions. The input traffic time series data first undergoes spatiotemporal attention mechanism to obtain the spatiotemporal correlation matrix. The TCM module introduces dilated convolutions to effectively handle long time series problems. The GCN module uses Chebyshev polynomial as the convolution kernel to reduce the computational complexity.

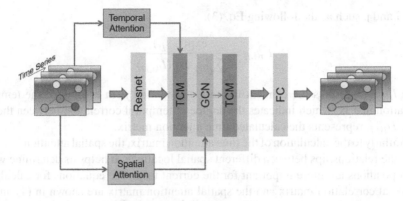

a. General Framework

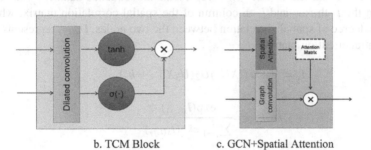

b. TCM Block   c. GCN+Spatial Attention

Fig. 1. ARSTGCN model framework

2.3 Spatiotemporal Attention Mechanism

The spatiotemporal attention mechanism [16] is a mechanism used to handle spatiotemporal data. It can learn and capture the correlations between different locations and time points in spatiotemporal data, thereby extracting and expressing important spatiotemporal features.

The temporal attention is used to model the relationships between different time points. It helps us determine which time points are more important for the current task. In time series data, the temporal attention mechanism can learn the evolution and variation patterns of different time points, as well as their impact on specific tasks. The temporal correlation matrix is defined as Eq. (2).

$$I_t = V_t \cdot \sigma\left(\left(X^T W_1\right) W_2(W_3 X) + b_t\right) \tag{2}$$

In the equations, $V_t, b_t \in R^{T \times T}$, $W_1 \in R^N, W_2 \in R^{F \times N}, W_3 \in R^F$ are the learnable parameters. $X \in R^{N \times F \times T}$ represents all sequence data, where N is the number of nodes, F is the number of data types, and T is the length of time. σ denotes the activation function. Based on the temporal correlation matrix, we calculate the time attention matrix between nodes i and j. such as the following Eq. (3).

$$I'_{t(i,j)} = \frac{\exp(I_{t(i,j)})}{\sum_{j=1}^{N} \exp(I_{t(i,j)})} \tag{3}$$

where $I_{t(i,j)}$ represents the element in the i -th row and j -th column of the temporal correlation matrix, which indicates the degree of temporal correlation between the two nodes. $I'_{t(i,j)}$ represents the calculated time attention matrix.

Similarly to the calculation of the time attention matrix, the spatial attention is used to model the relationships between different spatial locations. It helps us determine which spatial positions are more important for the current task. The equations for calculating the spatial correlation matrix and the spatial attention matrix are shown in (4) and (5) respectively. In these equations, V_s, $b_s \in R^{N \times N}$, $U_1 \in R^T$, $U_2 \in R^{F \times T}$, $U_3 \in R^F$ are all parameters to be learned, $X \in R^{N \times F \times T}$ represents all sequence data. $I_{s(i,j)}$ denotes the element in the i -th row and j -th column of the spatial correlation matrix, which represents the degree of spatial correlation between the two nodes. $I'_{s(i,j)}$ represents the calculated spatial attention matrix.

$$I_s = V_s \cdot \sigma((XU_1)U_2(U_3X)^T + b_s) \tag{4}$$

$$I'_{s(i,j)} = \frac{\exp(I_{s(i,j)})}{\sum_{j=1}^{N} \exp(I_{s(i,j)})} \tag{5}$$

2.4 Time Convolution

Recurrent neural networks have significant advantages in handling time series problems. However, they can suffer from the issues of vanishing and exploding gradients when dealing with long time series data. In addition, when dealing with complex problems, it requires adding multiple layers of convolution to capture the long-term dependencies in the time series. Dilated convolution [17] has a major advantage in that it can increase the receptive field without introducing additional parameters and computational complexity. By introducing a dilation rate parameter, the receptive field of the convolution kernel can be expanded. This allows the network to capture both local detailed features and larger contextual information. Therefore, in this paper, dilated convolution is used to extract temporal dynamic correlations, and the network architecture is shown in Fig. 1b. Given the input time series data $X \in R^{N \times T \times F}$, where N is the number of nodes, T is the time steps, and F is the number of features, the temporal convolution is defined as Eq. (6).

$$TCM(X) = g(Conv(X)) \odot \sigma(Conv(X)) \tag{6}$$

where, $g(\cdot)$ and $\sigma(\cdot)$ represent the activation functions tanh and sigmoid, respectively. $Conv(\cdot)$ denotes one-dimensional dilated convolution, and $\odot$ represent Hadamard multiplication. After obtaining the temporal feature correlations through the temporal convolutional layer, the spatial features are learned using the graph convolutional layer.

2.5 Graph Convolution

Graph convolution is mainly used to capture spatial dependencies among different nodes in a graph. Graph Convolutional Networks (GCNs) implement convolutional operations on topological graphs based on graph theory [18]. In graph convolution, each node has its own feature vector and is connected to its neighboring nodes to form an adjacency relationship. The goal of graph convolution is to update the features of each node by incorporating the feature information from its neighboring nodes. In graph convolution, the first step is to transform the adjacency matrix into a Laplacian matrix, which is defined as Eq. (7).

$$L = I_N - D^{-\frac{1}{2}} A D^{-\frac{1}{2}} \tag{7}$$

In the equation, I_N is the $N \times N$ identity matrix, A is the adjacency matrix of the graph G, and D is the degree matrix of the adjacency matrix A. The Laplacian matrix L is subjected to eigendecomposition, which decomposes it into the form $L = \beta \Lambda \beta^T$. Here, Λ is a diagonal matrix containing the eigenvalues, and β is a matrix containing the corresponding eigenvectors. The obtained parameters are used to perform graph convolution on the input time series sequence, and the equation is as follows.

$$g_\theta * x = g(L)x = \beta \Theta(\Lambda) \beta^T X_{in} \tag{8}$$

$g_\theta *$ is the graph convolution operator. Due to the computational complexity of Eq. (8), Hammond [19] et al. proposed that using Chebyshev polynomials to effectively solve this problem. Therefore, Eq. (8) can be approximated and simplified to Eq. (9).

$$g_\theta * x = g(L)x \approx \sum_{k=0}^{K-1} \theta_k T_k(\tilde{L})x \tag{9}$$

$$\tilde{L} = \frac{2L}{\lambda_{max} - I_N} \tag{10}$$

where, θ_k represents trainable parameters, $T_k(\tilde{L})$ are the coefficients of the Chebyshev polynomials. The expression for $\tilde{L}$ is defined as Eq. (10). λ_{max} is the maximum eigenvalue of the Laplacian, and K is the size of the convolutional kernel. In order to effectively learn spatial-temporal correlations, attention is incorporated into the convolutional operation in this paper, as shown in Fig. 1c. Therefore, Eq. (9) is modified to Eq. (11).

$$g_\theta * x = g(L)x \approx \sum_{k=0}^{K-1} \theta_k \left(T_k\left(\tilde{L}\right) \odot I'_{s(i,j)} \right)x \tag{11}$$

3   Experiment and Result Analysis

3.1 Dataset

This experiment uses two publicly available datasets, namely PEMSD4 and PEMSD8. PEMSD4 and PEMSD8 are datasets from the Los Angeles area in California, USA. Table 1 provides detailed information about these datasets. The distinctive feature of these two datasets is that they have a relatively fine granularity, with a statistical time interval of 5 min for each data group. In this experiment, one hour of traffic flow data is taken as the historical time period to predict the future traffic information for the next hour, with 12 data records considered as one time step. The datasets are divided into training, validation, and testing sets with a ratio of 6:2:2, respectively. The input data is processed using the Z-score method.

Table 1. Dataset description.

Datasets	Nodes	Timesteps	Time frame
PEMSD4	307	16992	2018.1.1—2018.2.28
PEMSD8	170	17856	2016.7.1—2016.8.31

3.2 Experimental Setting

The experiment was conducted in a Windows system environment, using the PyTorch framework. The computer processor used was Intel(R) Core(TM) i5-1135G7 @ 2.40 GH, with CUDA 10 and Python 3.7.

In the experiment, the Adam optimizer was employed, with a learning rate of 0.001. The batch size was set to 32. To measure the predictive performance of different methods, the chosen evaluation metrics were Mean Absolute Error (MAE) and Root Mean Square Error (RMSE). Smaller values of these metrics indicate better prediction performance of the model. The formula are given as Eq. (12) and (13) below.

(1) Mean Absolute Error:

$$\text{MAE} = \frac{1}{n} \sum_{i=1}^{n} |\widehat{y_i} - y_i| \tag{12}$$

(2) Root Mean Square Error:

$$\text{RMSE} = \left(\frac{1}{n} \sum_{i=1}^{n} |\widehat{y_i} - y_i| \right)^{\frac{1}{2}} \tag{13}$$

In the equations, y_i represents the true traffic flow and $\widehat{y_i}$ represents the predicted traffic flow for the i-th sample, where n represents the number of samples.

3.3 Baselines

This study compares the proposed model with six benchmark models for traffic flow prediction.

(1) Historical Average: This is a simple traffic flow prediction model that uses the historical average to predict future traffic flow.

(2) LSTM: LSTM is a type of recurrent neural network model that can capture long-term dependencies in time series data. It is used for predicting future traffic flow.

(3) T-GCN: T-GCN is a traffic flow prediction model that combines temporal information and graph convolution. It can effectively learn the spatiotemporal relationships and evolution patterns of traffic flow for future predictions.

(4) STGCN: STGCN is a spatial-temporal method for traffic flow prediction. It leverages graph convolutional operations to model the spatial and temporal dependencies in traffic data.

(5) ASTGCN: ASTGCN is a traffic flow prediction model that utilizes attention mechanisms along with spatial and temporal graph convolutional networks.

(6) Graph WaveNet [20]: Graph WaveNet is a traffic flow prediction model based on graph convolutional neural networks and WaveNet.

3.4 Experimental Results

Table 2 displays the prediction results of various models for a 60-min prediction on the PEMSD4 and PEMSD8 datasets. The benchmark experimental results in this study referenced the experimental data from ASTGCN [13]. The performance of the ARST-GCN model showed improvement on both datasets. Compared to ASTGCN, the proposed model improved the MAE and RMSE metrics by 1.7%, 2.4%, 8.02%, and 3.6% on PEMSD4 and PEMSD8, respectively. Compared to STGCN, the proposed model achieved an improvement of 10.1%, 10.1%, 6.5%, and 1.2% on PEMSD4 and PEMSD8 for the MAE and RMSE metrics, respectively.

Table 2. Performance comparison of different methods for one-hour traffic prediction on PEMSD4 and PEMSD8

Dataset	Metric	HA	LSTM	T-GCN	STGCN	Graph WaveNet	ASTGCN	ARSTGCN
PEMSD4	MAE	36.76	36.76	28.04	25.15	25.45	23.00	22.59
	RMSE	54.14	45.82	41.21	38.29	39.70	35.28	34.39
PEMSD8	MAE	29.52	23.18	24.01	18.88	19.13	19.19	17.65
	RMSE	44.03	36.96	33.98	27.87	31.05	29.20	27.52

3.5 Run Time Comparison

In the experiment, the computational time of the proposed ARSTGCN model was compared with the benchmark models STGCN and ASTGCN on the two datasets. Since STGCN and ASTGCN involve stacking multiple layers in their network, it increases the computational complexity. In this study, some complex network layers were reduced in the proposed model. As shown in Fig. 2, it can be observed that compared to STGCN and ASTGCN models, the ARSTGCN model had the least computational time on both datasets, resulting in significant speed improvements.

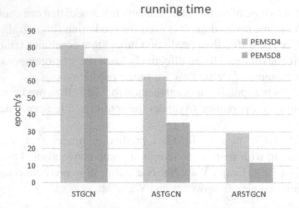

Fig. 2. Comparison of running times on dataset PEMSD4 and PEMSD8

4 Conclusion

This paper introduces the spatiotemporal attention mechanism to capture the temporal and spatial correlation respectively, reducing the defect of common graph convolution in extracting data features. Additionally, the paper introduces dilated convolutions to the existing benchmark models, which can increase the range of receptive fields without introducing extra parameters and computational complexity. This effectively solves the issues of gradient vanishing and explosion that often occur in long time series. This model is optimized in terms of network complexity, which not only improves accuracy but also greatly reduces time cost operations.

References

1. Tanimoto, J., An, X.: Improvement of traffic flux with introduction of a new lane-change protocol supported by intelligent traffic system. Chaos, Solitons Fractals: Interdisc. J. Nonlinear Sci. Nonequilibrium Complex Phenomena **122**, 1–5 (2019)
2. Smith, B.L., Williams, B.M., Oswald, R.K.: Comparison of parametric and nonparametric models for traffic flow forecasting. Transp. Res. Part C **10C**(4), 303–321 (2002)
3. Zivot, E., Wang, J.H.: Vector autoregressive models for multivariate time series. In: Modeling Financial Time Series with S-PLUS®, pp. 385–429 (2006). https://doi.org/10.1007/978-0-387-32348-0_11
4. Ahmed, M.S., Cook, A.R.: Analysis of freeway traffic time-series data by using box-jenkins techniques. Transp. Res. Rec. **722**, 1–9 (1979)
5. Okutani, I., Stephanedes, Y.J.:. Dynamic prediction of traffic volume through Kalman filtering theory. Transp. Res. Part B: Methodol. **18**(1), 1–11 (1984)
6. Vapnik, Vladimir. The nature of statistical learning theory. Springer science & business media, 1999
7. Xiaoli, Z., Guoguang, H., Huapu, L.: Short-term traffic flow prediction method based on k-neighborhood nonparametric regression. J. Syst. Eng. **24**(02), 178–183 (2009)
8. Ma, X., Tao, Z., Wang, Y., Yu, H., Wang, Y.: Long short-term memory neural network for traffic speed prediction using remote microwave sensor data. Transp. Res. Part C **54**, 187–197 (2015)

9. Yao, H., Wu, F., Ke, J., et al.: Deep multi-view spatial-temporal network for taxi demand prediction. In: Proceedings of the AAAI Conference on Artificial Intelligence, vol. 32, no. 1 (2018)

10. Bruna, J., Zaremba, W., Szlam, A., et al.: Spectral networks and locally connected networks on graphs. In: 2nd International Conference on Learning Representations, ICLR 2014, Banff, AB, Canada, 14–16 April, 2014, Conference Track Proceedings, pp. 1–10 (2014)

11. Li, Y., Yu, R., Shahabi, C., Liu, Y.: Diffusion convolutional recurrent neural network: data-driven traffic forecasting. In: Proceedings of the 6th International Conference on Learning Representations, pp. 1295–1302 (2018)

12. Yu, B., Yin, H., Zhu, Z.: Spatio-temporal graph convolutional networks: a deep learning framework for traffic forecasting. In: Proceedings of the 27th International Joint Conference on Artificial Intelligence, pp. 3634–3640 (2018)

13. Guo, S., Lin, Y., Feng, N., Song, C., Wan, H.: Attention based spatial-temporal graph convolutional networks for traffic flow forecasting. In: Proceedings of the 33th AAAI Conference on Artificial Intelligence, pp. 922–929 (2019)

14. Geng, X., Li, Y., Wang, L.: Spatiotemporal multi-graph convolution network for ride hailing demand forecasting. In: Proceedings of the 33th AAAI Conference on Artificial Intelligence, vol. 33, pp. 3656–3663 (2019)

15. Tedjopurnomo, D.A., Bao, Z.F., Zheng, B.H., et al.: A survey on modern deep neural network for traffic prediction: trends, methods and challenges. IEEE Trans. Knowl. Data Eng. **34**(4), 1544–1561 (2022)

16. Li, Y., et al.: Transformer with sparse attention mechanism for industrial time series forecasting. J. Phys. Conf. Ser. **2026**(1), 012036 (2021)

17. Yu, F., Koltun, V.: Multi-scale context aggregation by dilated convolutions. In: 4th International Conference on Learning Representations, San Juan, ICLR, pp. 1–13 (2016)

18. Kipe, T.N., Welling, M.: Semi-supervised classification with graph convolutional networks. In: 5th International Conference on Learning Repre sentations. Toulon:ICLR, pp. 1–14 (2017)

19. David, A., Hammond, K., VB, P., Remi Gribonval, C.: Wavelets on graphs via spectralgraph theory. Appl. Comput. Harmonic Anal. **30**(2), 129–150 (2011)

20. Wu, Z., Pan, S., Long, G., et al.: Graph WaveNet for deep spatial-temporal graph modeling. CoRR, abs/1906.00121 (2019)

Application Track

Design and Implementation of IoT-Enabled Intelligent Fire Detection System Using Neural Networks

Akram A. Almohammedi[1], Mohammed Balfaqih[2]([⊠]), Sohaib Nahas[2],
Abdullah Bokhari[2], and Abdulaziz Alqudsi[2]

[1] Electrical and Electronics Department, Karabük University, Karabük, Turkey
akramalzaghir@karabuk.edu.tr
[2] Department of Computer and Network Engineering, University of Jeddah, Jeddah,
Saudi Arabia
mabalfaqih@uj.edu.sa

Abstract. Fire detection systems are considered an integral part of any building. However, most fire detection systems use a single passive sensor that usually faces some unavoidable problems, especially with the use of simple processing systems using threshold and trend algorithms. Although more than a single sensor and fire information are used in some existing systems, the real-time fire information and firefighting forecasting are not monitored. Such information facilitates good decision making in firefighting and rescue operations. This paper develops a fast and smart fire detection and monitoring system that can detect and monitor fire incidents with low probability of detection error. The system involves IoT sensors that detect all necessary fire information including heating release rate smoke level, and CO_2 level. Moreover, a fire detection and monitoring model based on artificial neural networks is developed to identify fire information in real-time. The proposed system was tested in a chamber box with around 20 experiments. The positive fire detection rate was high with fast fire detection rate.

Keywords: Building fire · Internet of Things · Deep learning · Smart firefighting · Fire alarm

1 Introduction

Saudi Civil Defense reported that the number of fire incidents increases in the past five years in all regions of Saudi and reaches to more than 42,000 incidents in which more than 68% represents home fires [1]. Moreover, it is reported that the total material losses from fire accidents during 2021 exceeds 521 million riyals compared to more than 131 million riyals during 2020 [1]. Interestingly, the worldwide problem of safeguarding against fires and the financial repercussions associated with them is estimated to have a significant impact, with the average cost estimated to be around 1% of the annual global GDP. This expense tends to rise in correlation with the per capita GDP and human development index, as reported in [2]. This necessitates the need for concerted efforts from all authorities to reduce these losses by providing safety systems, firefighting equipment, and alarm devices.

© The Author(s), under exclusive license to Springer Nature Switzerland AG 2023
Y. Yang et al. (Eds.): AIMS 2023, LNCS 14202, pp. 63–70, 2023.
https://doi.org/10.1007/978-3-031-45140-9_6

Fire detection systems are considered an integral part of any building. Internet of Things (IoT) technology has been widely employed in fire detection systems over the last decade. However, most fire detection systems typically use a single passive sensor that faces problems with simple processing systems using threshold and trend algorithms. For instance, photosensitive detectors may be affected by sunlight and lighting, while smoke detectors may be affected by various gases. As a result, traditional fire detection systems can result in false fire alarms or require leak-checks. Although more than a single sensor and fire information are used in some existing systems, the real-time fire information and firefighting forecasting are not monitored. Such information facilitates good decision making in firefighting and rescue operations. Making effective firefighting decisions outside the fire scene is challenging without knowledge of the fire state.

Recently, ANN has been employed in fire research to support smart firefighting in various aspects [3–5]. In [6], the authors proposed a fire detection system that uses four sensors to detect fire, flame, smoke, and butane. Upon detecting a fire, the system sends data to an Arduino device which then sends a text message to notify the entity and stores the data for monthly or weekly inventory. The authors also created a mobile application to update the device and monitor its status. The Nashrek application, an open-source web application, was used to monitor the fire through the application. They utilized the MQ5 sensor to detect gas, smoke, or butane.

Cheng et al. [7] designed a fire detection device that uses gas, smoke, and CO_2 sensors, along with a neural network-based fire detection method [8]. The method has a low false alarm rate of less than 5% and can analyze sensor data sets in real-time. The system can adapt to its environment and accurately predict fires. However, accuracy may be impacted when implemented in a real-world setting. The system was tested in a simulator using MATLAB. An intelligent fire detection system with automatic water sprinklers was developed in [9], which utilized Wi-Fi devices and sensors as transmitters for sensor readings, including gas and flame sensors. Gas, temperature, and flame sensors were installed in the room, and the flame sensor could detect light in a specific range of wavelengths up to 33 cm.

The authors in [10] developed a fire detection system that uses a sensor board with 12 off-the-shelf sensors. These sensors include electrochemical gas sensors for CO detection, NDIR sensors for CO_2 detection, and PID and MOX sensors for VOC detection. Additionally, the system features a temperature and humidity sensor that connects to an Arduino DUE. The accuracy of the system was confirmed through successful experiments conducted in all temperatures and types of gases.

A fire system utilizing the Dynamic Time Warping Kernel Function was presented in [11]. It utilizes SVM-DTWK with a Multi-Modeling Approach and SVM classifier to accurately detect fires and minimize misclassifications. The system utilizes CO_2, temperature, smoke, and photoelectric sensors, and experiments were conducted to confirm its accuracy. In [12], the authors developed a system that utilizes a wireless sensor network and IoT to monitor the indoor environment's humidity, temperature, and CO_2 levels to prevent respiratory distress. Similarly, [13] designed a system based on the IoT to measure humidity, temperature, and light intensity.

Most of the existing systems employ a single sensor and simple detection algorithm which led to high false alarm rates and leak-checks. Complex fire detection systems that use temperature, smoke, and combustion sensors to overcome the limitations of simple fire detection systems have been introduced. However, simple processing algorithms were employed such as threshold and trend algorithms which reduces the accuracy of these systems. Moreover, Real-time fire information was not considered although it is crucial for effective firefighting and rescue operations. The importance of real-time fire detection and prediction in firefighting, evacuation, and rescue has been emphasized by numerous fire incidents, particularly in high-risk facilities and infrastructures.

This paper presents a fast and smart fire detection system that can detect and monitor fire incidents with low probability of detection error. The important contributions of this work are summarized as follows: 1) Design and implementation of an IoT-enabled intelligent fire detection system using neural networks. The IoT sensors developed in this paper can detect all necessary fire information including heating release rate, smoke level, and CO_2 level. 2) Development of a fire detection and monitoring model based on artificial neural networks to identify fire information in real-time. 3) Testing of the proposed system in a chamber box with around 20 experiments, which showed a high positive fire detection rate with fast fire detection rate.

2 IoT-Enabled Intelligent Fire Detection System

This section provides detailed explanation of the architecture of the proposed fire detection system. A detailed sequence diagram explaining the workflow of the proposed system is also presented.

2.1 System Architecture

The architecture of the smart fire detection system is composed of four main layers, as illustrated in Fig. 1, which are acquisition, communication, processing, and application layers. In the acquisition layer, the system employs a group of sensors to acquire fire related data. The sensors included in this layer are flame sensor, thermal sensor, smoke sensor, and CO_2 sensor. In the communication layer, the acquired data are sent to the cloud using cellular network. The fire incidents detection is obtained in accordance with acquired sensors data. The data are sent to the for the user to call authorities such as firefighters and healthcare providers.

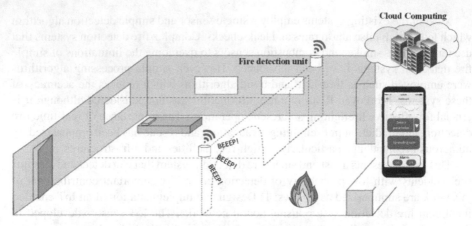

Fig. 1. Architecture of the Proposed Fire Detection System

2.2 Detailed Sequence Diagram

The detailed sequence diagram of the proposed fire detection system is shown in Fig. 2. The sensors readings are sent to the microcontroller to obtain the farm real time data including heat release rate, smoke level, and CO_2 level. All these data are forwarded to the cloud to store it. The data can be managed and stored in a standardized format by the server, which can then be accessed by the fire detection model. The microcontroller notifies, through the cloud and the platform, the user if any of the readings are not received to maintain and replace it. The fire detection model detects the fire incident occurrence. If the fire incident is detected, a buzzer alarm is turned on to warn the residents about the fire. Moreover, a fire alarm message will be sent to the user and the cloud to perform any further analysis required. However, to consider the fire put out, the buzzer will be turned off when the readings return to normal.

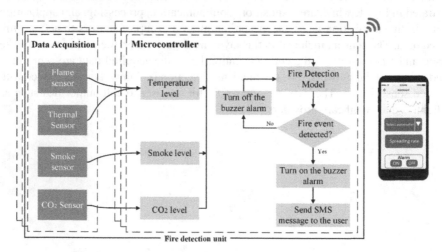

Fig. 2. Detailed sequence diagram of the fire detection system.

2.3 Dataset Generation

To develop the fire detection model, the initial phase involves creating a large and dependable dataset with a reasonable distribution of data that will be utilized for both training and validation of the model. For this purpose, Pyrosim and Fire Dynamic Simulator (FDS) is employed as they are efficient and save time in generating a large dataset that adheres to physical laws. Previous studies have confirmed the accuracy and feasibility of the numerical fire data produced by these tools [14–16]. Several parameters are required to be set to establish the numerical model including scenario geometries, material of the walls, mesh size, wall thickness, fire geometry, and fire source. To alert about fire incidents and guide firefighting strategies, critical indicators for building fire scenarios include spreading rate, coordinates, smoke level, and HRR as well as the level oCO_2f. Figure 3 shows the process of dataset generation.

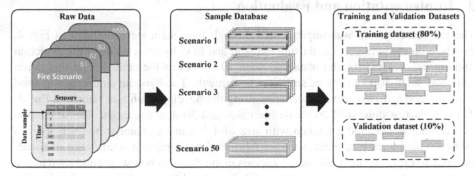

Fig. 3. Dataset generation process.

To create the dataset, a 2×4 matrix of eight fire detection units is installed on the ceiling with a distance of 10 cm between them. The fire simulation run for at least 300 s to allow the fire to reach a quasi-stable state. Simulating fire scenes with multiple sources of fire can be especially dangerous for firefighters, therefore only scenarios with one or two fire sources will be generated. The dataset comprises 50 fire scenarios, 20 of which are single fire cases, and the remaining 30 are dual fire cases with different fire characteristics. The data recorded in the datasheet for each simulation will be an 8×121 matrix (8 fire detection units by 121 simulation steps).

The dataset will be divided into 121 segments with a temporal length of 3 s each. The resulting dataset will contain 60,050 samples created by multiplying these segments by the number of scenarios. To train the fire detection model, each input data point in the dataset will be associated with an expected output [17]. This includes the fire's HRR, Smoke Level (SL), CO_2 Level (COL), Spreading Rate (SR), and x, y coordinates, expressed as the following vector:

$$[HRR_1, SL_1, COL_1, SR_1, x_1, y_1, HRR_2, SL_2, COL_2, SR_2, x_2, y_2]$$

where the subscript i = 1, 2 is the number of the fire source. The input data for the fire detection model will be labeled according to the simulation conditions, including HRR,

SL, COL, SR, and coordinates for each fire source. The second fire source values will be set to zero for a single fire case. The data will be shuffled randomly and split into training and validation datasets with ratios of 80% and 10%, respectively.

2.4 Fire Detection Model

The Convolutional Long Short-Term Memory (ConvLSTM) neural network will be utilized to recognize the fire information in an unfamiliar scenario. The considered parameters for the neural network are the relationship between the sensor data and the fire source information. This model will be constructed based on the dataset generated by the simulator. The ConvLSTM network is chosen due to its ability to extract features from spatial-temporal data [18]. The network will be developed using TensorFlow Core v2.2.0, following the approach outlined in [19].

3   Implementation and Evaluation

The proposed system was implemented through four main steps outlined in Fig. 4. Firstly, a dataset was generated using Pyrosim and FDS by arraying eight fire detection units in a 2 × 4 matrix and installing them 10 cm below the ceiling. The simulation time was set to 500 s to ensure sufficient fire growth. The Pyrosim simulator was used to create and test two primary scenarios using the developed unit, as shown in Fig. 5. These scenarios consist of 20 single fire cases and 30 dual fire cases. The simulation experiments considered a kitchen with size of 4 * 5 m. A chamber box was used to fabricate the room. Fire incidents were fabricated by burning a small piece of tissue. Around 20 experiments in different locations in the chamber box were conducted to test the developed system. The fire event was fabricated in different locations in the chamber box to examine the performance.

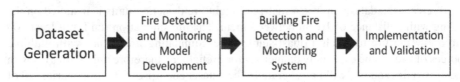

Fig. 4. Pyrosim Dataset generation process.

Then, the model is built based on the dataset generated by the simulator to determine the targeted fire information in a realistic fire environment. Colab notebook was employed to use TensorFlow to build the fire detection model as presented in [19]. In parallel, the smart fire detection unit was constructed. Upon detecting the fire event, a message is sent to the user containing the fire information including number of fire events, fire coordination, and spreading rate. Figure 6 shows the scenarios of two and single fire cases and Arduino IDE interface. Since the system is tested in the chamber, the accuracy of fire detection was high. The positive alarm rate was 100%. However, the fire dimensions were not accurate since the dimensions of a room with size of 4 * 5 m was considered. The speed of fire detection was around 0.5 s which is too low since the chamber box was used.

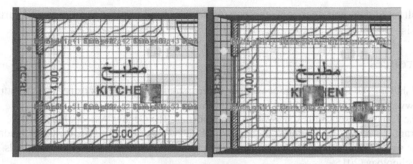

Fig. 5. Single and dual fire cases in Pyrosim

Fig. 6. Single and dual fire cases and Arduino IDE interface.

4   Conclusion

A smart fire detection system that can detect fire incidents with low probability of detection error was developed in this paper. To accomplish this, the following sub-objectives were achieved which are designing and developing IoT system that considers all necessary fire information including temperature, smoke level, and CO_2 level, as well as developing fire detection model based on artificial neural networks identify fire information in real-time. The proposed system was tested inside a chamber box with around 20 experiments. The positive fire detection rate was high with fast fire detection rate. However, this could be because the system was not tested in an open room. Moreover, it results in a wrong fire coordination finding. Hence, our future work is to test the system in an open room with bigger fire event size to obtain more realistic results. In addition, one fire spreading rate was considered in the model, hence, the developed model could be enhanced by predicting fire spreading rate. Application and/or website platforms can be developed in the future work to notify the user with fire data. All the collected data and decisions can be sent to the cloud server for storage and further analysis.

References

1. Alshallan, A.: Fires and their economic repercussions. Alriyadh newspaper (2022). https://www.alriyadh.com/1968905. Accessed 23 Nov 2022
2. The Geneva Association Staff: World Fire Statistics, The Geneva Association (2014)
3. Grant, C., Grant, C., Hamins, A., Bryner, N., Jones, A., Koepke, G.: Research roadmap for smart fire fighting. US Department of Commerce, National Institute of Standards and Technology (2015)
4. Naser, M.Z.: Mechanistically informed machine learning and artificial intelligence in fire engineering and sciences. Fire Technol. **57**(6), 2741–2784 (2021)
5. Huang, X., Wu, X., Usmani, A.: Perspectives of using artificial intelligence in building fire safety. In: Naser, M., Corbett, G. (eds.) Handbook of Cognitive and Autonomous Systems for Fire Resilient Infrastructures, pp. 139–159. Springer, Cham (2022). https://doi.org/10.1007/978-3-030-98685-8_6
6. Baba, M.C., Grado, J.J.B., Solis, D.J.L., Roma, I.M., Dellosa, JT.: A multisensory arduino-based fire detection and alarm system using GSM communications and RF module with an android application for fire monitoring. Int. J. Innov. Sci. Res. Technol. (IJISRT), 964–968. www.ijisrt.com. ISSN-2456-2165. https://doi.org/10.5281/zenodo, 6433836
7. Cheng, C., Sun, F., Zhou, X.: One fire detection method using neural networks. Tsinghua Sci. Technol. **16**(1), 31–35 (2011)
8. Zhairui, G., Zhengyu, F.: An algorithm of neural network for fire detection. Microcomput. Appl. **19**(11), 37–38 (2003)
9. Alqourabah, H., Muneer, A., Fati, S.M.: A smart fire detection system using IoT technology with automatic water sprinkler. Int. J. Electr. Comput. Eng. (2088-8708) **11**(4) (2021)
10. Solórzano, A., et al.: Early fire detection based on gas sensor arrays: multivariate calibration and validation. Sens. Actuators B Chem. **352**, 130961 (2022)
11. Baek, J., et al.: Real-time fire detection algorithm based on support vector machine with dynamic time warping kernel function. Fire Technol. **57**(6), 2929–2953 (2021)
12. Jiang, H., Li, Y., Li, D.: Indoor environment monitoring system based on linkit one and yeelink platform. In: 2016 2nd IEEE International Conference on Computer and Communications (ICCC), pp. 933–937. IEEE, October 2016
13. Rodrigues, M.J., Postolache, O., Cercas, F.: Indoor air quality monitoring system to prevent the triggering of respiratory distress. In: 2019 International Conference on Sensing and Instrumentation in IoT Era (ISSI), pp. 1–6. IEEE, August 2019
14. Wang, Z., Zhang, T., Huang, X.: Numerical modeling of compartment fires: ventilation characteristics and limitation of Kawagoe's law. Fire Technol., 1–24 (2022)
15. Wang, Z., Zhang, T., Huang, X.: Predicting real-time fire heat release rate by flame images and deep learning. In: Proceedings of the Combustion Institute (2022)
16. Tam, W.C., et al.: Generating synthetic sensor data to facilitate machine learning paradigm for prediction of building fire hazard. Fire Technol., 1–22 (2020)
17. Wang, D., Yang, Y., Ning, S.: DeepSTCL: a deep spatio-temporal ConvLSTM for travel demand prediction. In: 2018 International Joint Conference on Neural Networks (IJCNN), pp. 1–8. IEEE, July 2018
18. Azad, R., Asadi-Aghbolaghi, M., Fathy, M., Escalera, S.: Bi-directional ConvLSTM U-Net with densley connected convolutions. In: Proceedings of the IEEE/CVF International Conference on Computer Vision Workshops, p. 0 (2019)
19. Zhang, T., Wang, Z., Zeng, Y., Wu, X., Huang, X., Xiao, F.: Building Artificial-Intelligence Digital Fire (AID-Fire) system: a real-scale demonstration. J. Build. Eng. **62**, 105363 (2022)

Integrating State-of-the-Art Face Recognition and Anti-Spoofing Techniques into Enterprise Information Systems

Satyam Mishra[1] , Nguyen Thi Bich Thuy[2], and Cong-Doan Truong[1]

[1] International School, Vietnam National University, Hanoi, Vietnam
satyam.entrprnr@gmail.com, tcdoan@vnu.edu.vn
[2] University of Science, Vietnam National University, Hanoi, Vietnam
nguyenthibichthuy@hus.edu.vn

Abstract. Face Recognition Technology and Face Anti-Spoofing became a necessity during the Covid 19 pandemic, Monkeypox Virus etc. In the current era, the use of contactless technology has become crucial and highly beneficial for individuals. Vietnam is experiencing a significant digital transformation across various sectors including culture, education, tourism, finance, industry, and entertainment. However, most Enterprise Information System institutions in Vietnam lack facial recognition. To address this issue, we have undertaken research to devise a secure anti-spoofing method and determine an effective approach for face recognition processing. Our aim is to develop a comprehensive solution that can be implemented to establish a complete system that we researched and assessed at each stage. To construct a Facial Recognition application, we implemented a Convolutional Neural Network (CNN) as a core to recognize faces in real-time. To identify whether the faces are genuine or counterfeit, we utilized Landmark68 during the anti-spoofing phase. We applied our findings and developed an application AILib during the Covid-19 outbreak, when it was challenging for people to physically visit and login with their IDs at the counter. People can now login without physically being there by logging in using their faces on the AILib. According to the findings of our research, the system functions satisfactorily, with an ideal level of accuracy of 98.42%. Furthermore, we discovered that the optimal threshold value for identifying Asian faces in our face recognition test was determined to be 0.4, while varying threshold values were determined for different face types. For anti-spoofing, during the facial anti-spoofing test, the best threshold value for left, right and front was d < −50, d < −150 and d > −50 respectively, and the right value is d > −50 and in comparison, with state-of-the-art methods is pretty good. The program has a high level of practicality, significantly advancing the groundbreaking application of artificial intelligence to enhance people's quality of life and safety.

Keywords: Face Recognition Technology (FRT) · Anti-Spoofing · CNN (Convolutional Neural Network) · Face Landmark/Landmark68

Y. Yang et al. (Eds.): AIMS 2023, LNCS 14202, pp. 71–84, 2023.
https://doi.org/10.1007/978-3-031-45140-9_7

1 Introduction

Face recognition technology (FRT) is a biometric picture capturing tool that's utilized for either identity verification or to recognize an individual to associate them absolutely to their recorded information [1]. For instance, it is frequently employed at the entrances of airport security checkpoints. Although this particular use has its benefits in terms of improved efficiency, its effectiveness relies on the system's processing capability and its specific application [2]. Attendance access control is where face recognition technology finds its widest application in terms of its implementation design [3], security [4] and finance, The areas where face recognition technology is utilized include logistics, retail, smartphones, transportation, education, real estate, government administration, entertainment promotion, and network information security [5–7] and Additional sectors are starting to incorporate face recognition technology. In the realm of security, both the early detection of suspicious incidents and the tracking of suspects can be effectively carried out with the aid of facial recognition [8]. In the field of face recognition technologies and related technologies, there are several stages of development, three of which will be discussed here. The first stage is the Early Algorithm Stage, which includes Principal Component Analysis (PCA) and Linear Discriminant Analysis (LDA) [9]. Among these algorithms, PCA is widely recognized as the most commonly used method for reducing data dimensionality [10–13]. The second stage, known as the Artificial Features and Classifiers Stage, incorporates various techniques such as Support Vector Machine (SVM), Adaboost, Small Samples, and Neural Networks. On the other hand, the final stage, Deep Learning, is a subset of machine learning that has revolutionized the face recognition industry. Unlike previous stages that require feature extraction, deep learning can automatically identify the necessary features for categorization during the training process. This advancement has had a profound impact on the field of face recognition [14]. Convolutional Neural Network (CNN) falls under one of the categories of face recognition technology. CNN incorporates elements such as localized perception areas, shared weights, and downsampling of facial images to enhance the model structure by leveraging the data's locality and other distinctive characteristics [15]. Some image processing techniques also involve canny edge detection algorithms, quite useful to detect wide range of edges in images [9].

Anti-spoofing refers to the measures taken to counteract spoofing attacks, which involve manipulating data in an attempt to impersonate someone else and gain unauthorized access [16]. The IJCB 2011 competition, which focused on countering 2D facial spoofing attacks, took place recently [17] was a significant group effort for identifying efficient methods for non-intrusive spoofing detection. Multi-modal analysis [18–20], challenge-response technique [21], and multispectral imaging [22] all offer effective ways to distinguish between real and fake faces, However, their practicality is limited due to the requirement for user interaction or specialized imaging requirements. Hence, there is a strong desire to incorporate anti-spoofing techniques into existing face authentication systems that eliminate the need for user cooperation and can utilize standard imaging equipment. One key aspect in verifying the authenticity of a face is the detection of eye blinks, and there are various automated methods available for identifying eye blinks in video frames. Typically, the Viola Jones [23] The operator is employed to detect facial features and landmarks, followed by the utilization of adaptive thresholding to calculate the optical flow surrounding the eyes. Ultimately, by employing a correlation matching template for both open and closed eyes, the eye's motion is estimated.

Since early 2020, the COVID-19 pandemic, triggered by the emergence of the novel SARS-CoV-2 coronavirus, has afflicted the world. Throughout this prolonged period of the pandemic, contactless applications can be implemented by leveraging Face Recognition Technology [24–27]. Amidst the ongoing pandemic, the utilization of Face Recognition technology proves highly beneficial. It eliminates the need for physical presence of students for authentication and allows teachers to mark attendance without having to touch fingerprint scanners. Thang Long University in Vietnam has taken the initiative to test this technology for attendance purposes in classrooms. Their specific face recognition technology, known as "TLnet," automatically identifies and records the faces of students in class [28]. Similarly, Vconnex smart home company launched its face recognition smart lock product which involves face recognition login but lacks security of being spoofed [29]. However, these particular application lacks the capability to prevent face spoofing.

Moreover, in the majority of Enterprise Information System institutions in Vietnam, facial recognition and anti-spoofing technology are not implemented, resulting in employees needing their identity cards to check-in instead of using their faces which is not contact less application; therefore, dangerous during pandemic times. After carefully examining these issues, we have put forth our research proposal to develop a comprehensive system. Our aim was to investigate and evaluate suitable methods for facial recognition processing and secure anti-spoofing measures. We utilized a Convolutional Neural Network (CNN) as the core component for building a real-time Facial Recognition application that detects faces, and incorporated Landmark68 for anti-spoofing to determine the authenticity of a face.

During the Covid-19 pandemic, when physical presence was challenging for people to log in with their IDs at the counter or entrance of Enterprise Information System Institutions, we implemented our research findings and created a user-friendly application called AILib. Now, people can log in to AILib using their faces, eliminating the need to be physically present. The system collects user facial data to enhance the accuracy of face recognition.

Based on our research results, the system has demonstrated satisfactory performance, achieving an optimal accuracy level of 98.42%. Furthermore, we discovered that the best threshold value for Asian faces during face recognition testing was 0.4, while different values applied to other face types. For anti-spoofing, the optimal threshold values for left, right, and front faces were found to be $d < -50$, $d < -150$, and $d > -50$, respectively. This algorithm can be practically applied, making a significant contribution to the innovative application of Artificial Intelligence in improving people's lives, making them safer and more secure.

This paper presents several noteworthy contributions:

a) Creation of a comprehensive system: The authors have developed and implemented a robust system called AILib, which combines facial recognition technology with reliable anti-spoofing measures. This innovative solution allows users to log in using their faces, eliminating the need for physical presence. Particularly during times like Covid-19 and Monkeypox outbreaks, this feature proves advantageous.

b) Utilization of Convolutional Neural Network (CNN) for face recognition: The authors have successfully incorporated CNN as the main component in their real-time face recognition application. This cutting-edge deep learning approach effectively detects crucial facial features without any human intervention.

c) Implementation of Face Landmark/Landmark68 for anti-spoofing: To ensure authenticity and prevent spoofing, the authors have employed the Face Landmark/Landmark68 technique. By analyzing facial landmarks, this system prompts users to perform random actions, making it extremely challenging for fake videos to be used for authentication.

d) Determination of optimal threshold values: Through extensive testing and analysis, the authors have identified ideal threshold values for both face recognition and anti-spoofing across different types of faces. For Asian faces specifically, a threshold value of 0.4 was found to be most effective for face recognition. Additionally, values such as $d < -50$ for left pose, $d < -150$ for right pose, and $d > -50$ for front pose were discovered to enhance anti-spoofing measures.

e) Practical implementation in real-world scenarios: The proposed system has been successfully implemented and rigorously tested in various real-world environments. These practical demonstrations showcase its potential to greatly improve people's lives by offering a secure and convenient authentication method.

2   Methodology

The proposed methodology's architecture as you can see in Fig. 1 comprises several key components. Let's take a closer look:

Front-end Client:

- This is a web-based interface that enables user interaction.
- It captures the user's face using the camera on their device.
- The captured face image is then sent to the back-end server for further processing.

Back-end Server:

- Upon receiving the user's face image from the front-end client, it begins real-time face detection using the Tiny Face Detector Model.
- Facial features are extracted from the detected face utilizing a Deep Convolutional Neural Network (CNN).
- These facial features are encoded into a vector representation, which is then matched with existing face encodings in the database.
- Additionally, it employs the Face Landmark/Landmark68 approach to detect and locate specific facial points such as eyes, nose, and mouth relative to the overall face structure.
- As an added security measure against spoofing attempts, users are prompted to perform random facial expressions like smiling or looking left/right.

Face Database:

- This component serves as a repository for storing and managing facial encodings of registered users.

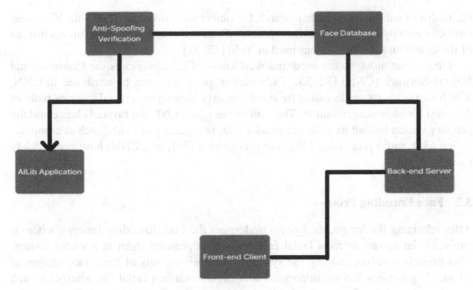

Fig. 1. Proposed Methodology Architecture

- During the face recognition process, these encodings are compared for identification purposes.

   Anti-Spoofing Verification:

- To ensure authenticity, this feature measures distances between specific facial points (e.g., point 36 and point 18, point 45 and point 25) in order to detect any noticeable facial movements or changes.
- It analyzes various aspects of facial expressions and movements to verify user authentication.

   AILib Application:

- This application provides a user-friendly platform for secure logins.
- Instead of relying on physical presence, users can conveniently log in using their unique facial features.
- Furthermore, regular collection of user facial data helps enhance accuracy over time.

3 Face Recognition Process

3.1 Face Detection

Face detection is a method used to identify the position and dimensions of a person's face within a digital image. It is the initial and crucial step in the process of face recognition. In our research, we utilized the Tiny Face Detector Model to achieve real-time face detection [30]. When it comes to clients with limited resources and mobile devices, our preferred face detector is the Tiny Face Detector. It is highly suitable for mobile platforms and web applications due to its exceptional mobility and compatibility. Additionally, in the realm of automated vehicle research for object detection, the Tiny Yolo V2 model has been employed. This model incorporates depth-wise separable convolutions instead of the conventional convolutions used in Yolo [25, 31].

One of the most widely used and well-known DL networks is the Convolutional Neural Network (CNN) [32, 33]. DL's current popularity can be attributed to CNN, which surpasses its predecessors by autonomously identifying crucial features without the need for human intervention. This ability has made CNN the favored choice and the primary reason behind its widespread adoption. In a variety of fields, such as computer vision [34], audio processing [35], face recognition [36], etc., CNNs have been widely used.

3.2 Face Encoding Process

After receiving the image, the system undergoes the Face Encoding Process, where it analyzes the image, extracts facial features, and represents them in a vector format. This process involves training the system by examining sets of three face images at a time. It generates 128 measurements that capture various facial characteristics such as color, size, slant of eyes, and the distance between eyebrows. To enhance accuracy, slight modifications are made to the neural network, ensuring that the measurements for Image 1 and Image 2 are closer together, while the measurements for Image 2 and Image 3 are further apart. This step is repeated millions of times for millions of images featuring thousands of individuals, allowing the network to consistently generate reliable 128 measurements for each person. Consequently, any set of ten different pictures of the same person should yield the same set of measurements [37].

4 Face Anti-Spoofing Method

4.1 Face Landmark/Landmark68

Facial Landmark refers to the identification of the eye, nose, and mouth's location relative to the overall facial structure. We will search for the primary points that constitute the object's shape within an image. This process consists of two steps: 1. Locating the face within the image, and 2. Detecting the facial structures. Although the face contains numerous key points, our focus will be on essential ones, namely the mouth, right eyebrow, left eyebrow, left eye, right eye, nose, and jaw. The system will utilize the "dlib" library as its foundation [38]. As shown in Fig. 2 below, this method will determine 68 key points that follow the (x, y) coordinates.

As the human face consists of 68 distinct points, any changes in the position of these points will result in a corresponding change in the distance between them. In our system, we leverage this method to prompt users to smile, look left, and look right. We introduce these requirements randomly to prevent users from creating fake videos. To calculate and identify facial movement, we utilize landmark data obtained through an API based on the "dlib" library's landmark. This library can detect the flow of 68 key points with (x, y) coordinates that constitute the human face. Figure 3 illustrates the three poses: frontal, left yaw, and right yaw.

Fig. 2. 68 key points in human face

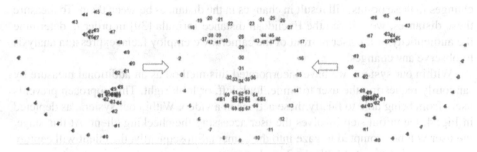

Fig. 3. Face Change Position

Using the face landmark API, we possess the x and y coordinates of 68 essential points on a person's face, each point having a unique value. By measuring the distance between these points, we can detect facial movement accurately. We use Euclidean distance [39] to calculate the distance between each point.

$$d(p, q) = \sqrt{(q1 - p1)^2 + (q2 - p2)^2}$$

Based on Euclidean distance, we can define when the face looks in front of the camera, turn left and turn right to check that the user in front of camera is a real person.

4.2 Face Expression

Two commonly employed approaches for comprehending human emotions involve the analysis of physical or sensory signals. Physical signals include facial expressions, speech, and gestures, while sensory signals contribute to the expression of six fundamental emotions [40]. We can detect the status of human expressions using landmarks and then use this information for various purposes, one of them is anti-spoofing as well. We will use Euclidean distance formula [39] to calculate distance changing from one point to other on facial landmark data to get the facial expression.

5 Proposed Process of Application

In summary, we utilized the Tiny Face Detector Model to detect faces in real-time. Once an image is received, the system begins analyzing it to extract facial features, transforming them into a vector representation. This involved training a Deep Convolutional Neural Network (DCNN) to generate precise measurements of facial features.

The training dataset consisted of three types of images: two images of the same person, two images of different people, and one image of a completely different person. After training, the network became proficient in generating 128 measurements for each person. The person's image stored in the database is then compared with the face image sent by the web client.

Additionally, we employed the Face Landmark/Landmark 68 approach to determine the position of the eyes, nose, and mouth relative to the face. This method involves two steps: first, locating the face in the image, and second, detecting the facial features. By determining the (x, y) coordinates, we establish 68 points on the human face. Any changes in these points will result in changes in the distances between them. To measure these distances, we utilized the Euclidean distance formula [39] in order to determine the authenticity of the user in front of the camera, we employ facial expression analysis to observe any changes.

Within our system, we have incorporated this method as an additional measure by randomly requesting the user to smile, look left, or look right. This approach prevents users from being able to falsify these actions in a video. Within our system, as depicted in Fig. 4, the initial step involves the user accessing the checking client. At this stage, the user will be prompted to gaze into the camera. Subsequently, the client will capture an image and transmit it to the back-end server.

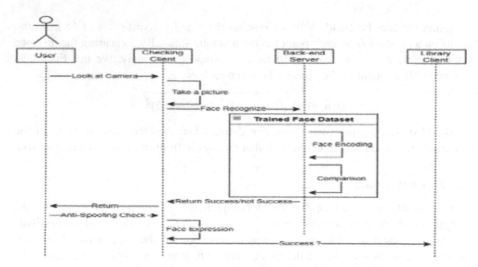

Fig. 4. System Use Case Diagram

This image will be passed to convolutional neural the network model is utilized for training purposes and subsequently, the system encodes the input image to extract facial measurements and compares them with the existing face encodings in the dataset. If the input image matches a pre-existing image, it proceeds to an anti-spoofing process. The user is then prompted to smile or perform a random expression, and once the facial expression is captured, the system verifies the anti-spoofing measures and allows successful login into the user's account on the AILib platform.

6 Results

6.1 Technologies Used

Our system has been specifically designed to incorporate face recognition and anti-spoofing measures. We have implemented face matching in various environments with different lighting conditions. For the front-end and back-end development, we utilized HTML, CSS, and JavaScript to create the web front-end, Python to build the back-end API, Flask as the web framework, and SQLite for storing user information. To enable face-related functionalities such as face detection, landmark68, face expression, and gender recognition, we employed NodeJS along with TensorFlow.js and face-api.js. To ensure accurate face detection and to prevent fake faces, we utilized the Tiny face detector model and landmark68. Additionally, the system underwent two stages of testing: the face recognition test and the face anti-spoofing test.

6.2 The Best Threshold for Application

6.2.1 Face Recognition Threshold Value

To determine the optimal threshold value for face recognition, we conducted two primary steps in a face recognition test: true authentication tests and false acceptance authentication tests. These tests aimed to identify the ideal threshold value and measure the time taken for face recognition. Each individual underwent verification by comparing images captured with various cameras under different lighting conditions. The face recognition time was assessed through 30 trials for each combination of templates and lighting configurations. We tested threshold values of 0.6, 0.55, 0.5, 0.45, and 0.4, repeating each test 100 times to determine the optimal value specifically for Asia Face.

During each trial, the system captured a single frame of face video, loaded the corresponding digital template, searched for a face, and compared it to the existing dataset to find a match. If a match was found, the trial saved the current accuracy before proceeding to the next image in the dataset. The trial concluded once all the subject's face images were scanned, and the highest accuracy achieved was recorded. If no match was found after scanning all the subject's images, the trial stopped and returned a success message stating "not found." In Fig. 4, the system displays the name of the user along with their accuracy and other relevant details when a face match is found.

We performed ten tests using the threshold test case, and for European faces, a tolerance of 0.6 yielded the best results, successfully recognizing individuals with only one to three pictures per subject. However, when applying face recognition to Asia Face, this approach was inaccurate. Table 1 presents the results recorded for face recognition with Asian Face. The system incorrectly recognized the input image when the threshold was set to 0.5 or 0.6. Setting the threshold below 0.5 yielded better results with no incorrect subject identifications. However, in some cases, we were unable to match any subject with a threshold value below 0.45.

We strive to ensure consistency by conducting the tests in the same environment. According to the findings in Table 1, the system with a tolerance of 0.4 is determined to be the most suitable for Asian faces. Figure 5 shows a successful user interface of our research implementation in AILib App.

Table 1. Detect Asian Face with threshold (W- Wrong, R- Right, NF- Not Found)

Threshold	0.6	0.55	0.5	0.45	0.4	0.35	0.3	0.25	0.2	0.1
Result	W	R	W	R	R	R	R	NF	NF	R
	R	W	W	R	R	R	R	NF	R	NF
	W	W	R	R	R	R	NF	R	NF	R
	R	W	R	R	R	R	NF	R	R	NF
	W	R	R	R	R	R	R	R	R	R
	W	R	R	W	R	R	R	R	NF	R
	W	W	W	R	R	NF	R	NF	R	NF
	W	W	W	R	R	R	R	R	R	R
	W	W	R	R	R	R	R	R	R	NF
	W	W	W	R	R	R	R	R	R	R

Fig. 5. System Encoding Face, performing anti-spoofing and displaying result

6.2.2 Face Anti-Spoofing Threshold Value

During the face anti-spoofing test, three digital templates were employed: the left face, the right face, and the smile face. These trials were conducted to assess the distance between various points on the face. Whenever the face position changed during a trial, the system recorded the values of each facial point within the 68-landmark model, including the distances between point 36 and point 18, point 45 and point 25, and point 63 and point 67.

Based on this, we have conducted calculations to determine the required distance for performing face anti-spoofing. Upon successful spoof checking, the Library Client application appears and displays the recognized user. In our testing, we performed ten trials using the threshold test case, and a tolerance of 0.6 yielded the best results for European faces. For each subject, successful face recognition was achieved with just one to three pictures. However, when it comes to Asian faces, the face recognition results were inaccurate.

Table 2. Value of d

	Left	Front (Smile)	Right
Value of d	−160	−78	−28
	−167	−58	−14
	−164	−56	5
	−178	−98	−39
	−171	−65	−41
	−156	−61	−20
	−167	−91	−44
	−157	−68	−34
	−173	−65	−31
	−155	−103	−15
	−160	−102	−47
	−165	−67	−20
	−153	−74	−45
	−175	−91	−46
	−185	−96	−31
	−188	−97	−43
	−173	−67	−36
	−175	−106	−18
	−178	−90	−42
	−151	−89	−46

In the face anti-spoofing test case, we measured the distance between point 36 and point 18, as well as the distance between point 45 and point 25. We then conducted tests to determine if we could detect the orientation of the face (left or right). As a result of this test case, we obtained three values: "l" represents the value between 36 and 18, "r" represents the value between 45 and 25, and "d" represents the difference between "l" and "r". After conducting ten tests, we recorded values corresponding to a face perpendicular to the camera (smile), a face looking left, and a face looking right. All these values are presented in Table 2.

After conducting 20 tests, we discovered that a front-facing face has a value of "d" less than −50, a left-facing face has a value of "d" less than −150, and a right-facing face has a value of "d" greater than −50. These results are quite favorable when compared to state-of-the-art methods.

7 Conclusion

Our extensive research aimed to develop a comprehensive system involved meticulous evaluation at each stage, focusing on identifying an appropriate facial recognition processing method and implementing a robust anti-spoofing technique. Our efforts were fruitful, resulting in the creation of the AILib application, which was particularly useful during the Covid-19 pandemic. People can now securely login by logging into AILib using their facial features, eliminating the need for physical presence—a particularly advantageous feature during pandemics such as Covid-19 and Monkeypox.

To enhance the accuracy of face recognition, our system collects user facial data. Based on our research findings, the system exhibits satisfactory performance, achieving an optimal accuracy level of 98.42%. Furthermore, we determined that the ideal threshold value for Asian faces during face recognition tests is 0.4, while different thresholds apply to other facial types. Regarding anti-spoofing, our facial anti-spoofing test identified threshold values of $d < -50$ for the left pose, $d < -150$ for the right pose, and $d > -50$ for the front pose.

Further improvements to our system's training and face recognition speed can be achieved by utilizing a client machine and a back-end server. This algorithmic solution holds practical applications and contributes significantly to the pioneering field of Artificial Intelligence, thereby promoting a better and safer way of life. Our research presents a valuable opportunity to modernize existing traditional login/authentication systems by providing users with a convenient and secure means of accessing and protecting their data.

References

1. Lin, S.-H.: An introduction to face recognition technology. Inf. Sci. Int. J. Emerg. Transdiscipl. **3**, 1–7 (2000)
2. Berle, I.: What is face recognition technology? In: Berle, I. (ed.) Face Recognition Technology: Compulsory Visibility and Its Impact on Privacy and the Confidentiality of Personal Identifiable Images, pp. 9–25. Springer, Cham (2020). https://doi.org/10.1007/978-3-030-368 87-6_2
3. Manjula, V., Baboo, L.: Face detection identification and tracking by PRDIT algorithm using image database for crime investigation. Int. J. Comput. Appl. **38**, 40–46 (2012). https://doi.org/10.5120/4741-6649
4. Lander, K., Bruce, V., Bindemann, M.: Use-inspired basic research on individual differences in face identification: implications for criminal investigation and security. Cogn. Res Princ. Implic. **3**, 26 (2018). https://doi.org/10.1186/s41235-018-0115-6
5. Hu, Y., An, H., Guo, Y., Zhang, C., Zhang, T., Ye, L.: The development status and prospects on the face recognition. In: 2010 4th International Conference on Bioinformatics and Biomedical Engineering, pp. 1–4 (2010). https://doi.org/10.1109/ICBBE.2010.5517197
6. Mishra, S., Vi, P.T., Phuc, V.M., Oni, D., Tanh, N.V.: Using security metrics to determine security program effectiveness. In: Human Factors in Cybersecurity. AHFE Open Acces (2023). https://doi.org/10.54941/ahfe1003720
7. Mishra, S., Phuc, V.M., Tanh, N.V.: Lightweight authentication encryption to improve DTLS, quark combined with overhearing to prevent DoS and MITM on low-resource IoT devices. In: Tekinerdogan, B., Wang, Y., Zhang, L.-J. (eds.) ICIOT 2022. LNCS, vol. 13735, pp. 108–122. Springer, Cham (2023). https://doi.org/10.1007/978-3-031-23582-5_8

8. Mishra, S., Phuc, V.M., Igbagbo, O.D.: BNIS- Bot Node Isolation Strategy to Prevent DoS Attacks: An Improved Overhearing Solution

9. Mishra, S., Thanh, L.T.: SATMeas - object detection and measurement: canny edge detection algorithm. In: Pan, X., Jin, T., Zhang, L.-J. (eds.) AIMS 2022. LNCS, vol. 13729, pp. 91–101. Springer, Cham (2022). https://doi.org/10.1007/978-3-031-23504-7_7

10. Hoyle, D.C., Rattray, M.: PCA learning for sparse high-dimensional data. Europhys. Lett. (EPL) **62**, 117–123 (2003). https://doi.org/10.1209/epl/i2003-00370-1

11. Vijay, K., Selvakumar, K.: Brain FMRI clustering using interaction K-means algorithm with PCA. In: 2015 International Conference on Communications and Signal Processing (ICCSP), pp. 0909–0913 (2015). https://doi.org/10.1109/ICCSP.2015.7322628

12. Vogt, F., Mizaikoff, B., Tacke, M.: Numerical methods for accelerating the PCA of large data sets applied to hyperspectral imaging. Presented at the Proceedings of the SPIE, 22 February (2002). https://doi.org/10.1117/12.456960

13. Ordonez, C., Mohanam, N., Garcia-Alvarado, C.: PCA for large data sets with parallel data summarization. Distrib. Parallel Databases **32**, 377–403 (2013). https://doi.org/10.1007/s10 619-013-7134-6

14. Wang, W., Yang, J., Xiao, J., Li, S., Zhou, D.: Face Recognition Based on Deep Learning. In: Zu, Q., Hu, B., Gu, N., Seng, S. (eds.) HCC 2014. LNCS, vol. 8944, pp. 812–820. Springer, Cham (2015). https://doi.org/10.1007/978-3-319-15554-8_73

15. Li, Y., Cha, S.: Implementation of robust face recognition system using live video feed based on CNN. arXiv preprint arXiv:1811.07339 (2018)

16. Schuckers, S.A.: Spoofing and anti-spoofing measures. Inf. Secur. Tech. Rep. **7**, 56–62 (2002)

17. Chakka, M.M. (eds.): Competition on Counter Measures to 2-D Facial Spoofing Attacks (2011). https://doi.org/10.1109/IJCB.2011.6117509

18. Chetty, G., Wagner, M.: Liveness verification in audio-video speaker authentication. In: Proceedings of the 10th ASSTA Conference, pp. 358–363. Macquarie University Press

19. Frischholz, R., Dieckmann, U.: BioID: a multimodal biometric identification system. Computer **33**, 64–68 (2000). https://doi.org/10.1109/2.820041

20. Kollreider, K., Fronthaler, H., Faraj, M.I., Bigun, J.: Real-time face detection and motion analysis with application in "liveness" assessment. IEEE Trans. Inf. Forensics Secur. **2**, 548–558 (2007). https://doi.org/10.1109/TIFS.2007.902037

21. De Marsico, M., Nappi, M., Riccio, D., Dugelay, J.-L.: Moving face spoofing detection via 3D projective invariants. In: 2012 5th IAPR International Conference on Biometrics (ICB), pp. 73–78 (2012). https://doi.org/10.1109/ICB.2012.6199761

22. Pavlidis, I., Symosek, P.: The imaging issue in an automatic face/disguise detection system. In: Proceedings IEEE Workshop on Computer Vision Beyond the Visible Spectrum: Methods and Applications (Cat. No.PR00640), pp. 15–24 (2000). https://doi.org/10.1109/CVBVS.2000. 855246

23. Viola, P., Jones, M.J.: Robust real-time face detection. Int. J. Comput. Vision **57**, 137–154 (2004)

24. Coronavirus disease (COVID-19) – World Health Organization. https://www.who.int/emerge ncies/diseases/novel-coronavirus-2019. Accessed 12 Aug 2022

25. Mishra, S., Minh, C.S., Thi Chuc, H., Long, T.V., Nguyen, T.T.: Automated robot (car) using artificial intelligence. In: 2021 International Seminar on Machine Learning, Optimization, and Data Science (ISMODE), pp. 319–324 (2022). https://doi.org/10.1109/ISMODE53584. 2022.9743130

26. Monkeypox cases are rising—here's what we know so far. https://www.nationalgeographic. com/science/article/monkeypox-cases-are-risingheres-what-we-know-so-far. Accessed 12 Aug 2022

27. Norstrom, P., Consulting, A.: Has Covid increased public faith in facial recognition? Biometric Technol. Today **2021**, 5–8 (2021). https://doi.org/10.1016/S0969-4765(21)00121-1

28. This is the first university in Vietnam to take attendance with face recognition, evasion is only in the past. https://tipsmake.com/this-is-the-first-university-in-vietnam-to-take-attend ance-with-face-recognition-evasion-is-only-in-the-past. Accessed 12 Aug 2022

29. News, V.: Báo VietnamNet. https://vietnamnet.vn/en/vietnamese-engineers-develop-face-rec ognition-smart-lock-2132161.html. Accessed 29 June 2023

30. Hu, P., Ramanan, D.: Finding Tiny Faces (2017). http://arxiv.org/abs/1612.04402

31. Yap, J.W., bin Mohd Yussof, Z., bin Salim, S.I., Lim, K.C.: Fixed point implementation of Tiny-Yolo-v2 using OpenCL on FPGA. Int. J. Adv. Comput. Sci. Appl. (IJACSA) **9** (2018). https://doi.org/10.14569/IJACSA.2018.091062

32. Yao, G., Lei, T., Zhong, J.: A review of Convolutional-Neural-Network-based action recognition. Pattern Recogn. Lett. **118**, 14–22 (2019). https://doi.org/10.1016/j.patrec.2018. 05.018

33. Dhillon, A., Verma, G.K.: Convolutional neural network: a review of models, methodologies and applications to object detection. Prog. Artif. Intell. **9**, 85–112 (2020). https://doi.org/10. 1007/s13748-019-00203-0

34. Fang, W., Love, P.E.D., Luo, H., Ding, L.: Computer vision for behaviour-based safety in construction: a review and future directions. Adv. Eng. Inform. **43**, 100980 (2020). https:// doi.org/10.1016/j.aei.2019.100980

35. Palaz, D., Magimai-Doss, M., Collobert, R.: End-to-end acoustic modeling using convolutional neural networks for HMM-based automatic speech recognition. Speech Commun. **108**, 15–32 (2019). https://doi.org/10.1016/j.specom.2019.01.004

36. Li, H.-C., Deng, Z.-Y., Chiang, H.-H.: Lightweight and resource-constrained learning network for face recognition with performance optimization. Sensors **20**, 6114 (2020). https://doi.org/ 10.3390/s20216114

37. Machine Learning is Fun! Part 4: Modern Face Recognition with Deep Learning. https://med ium.com/@ageitgey/machine-learning-is-fun-part-4-modern-face-recognition-with-deep-learning-c3cffc121d78

38. face-api.js. https://justadudewhohacks.github.io/face-api.js/docs/index.html#models-face-landmark-detection. Accessed 13 Aug 2022

39. Liberti, L., Lavor, C., Maculan, N., Mucherino, A.: Euclidean distance geometry and applications. SIAM Rev. **56**, 3–69 (2014). https://doi.org/10.1137/120875909

40. How to Read Body Language and Facial Expressions. https://www.verywellmind.com/und erstand-body-language-and-facial-expressions-4147228. Accessed 13 Aug 2022

The Load Forecasting of Special Transformer Users Based on Unsupervised Fusion Model

Yuanyang Tang[1]([✉]), Liang Yu[1], Zhenjiang Pang[1], Haimin Hong[2], Zhaowu Zhan[1], Chengwen Zhao[1], Minglang Wu[1], and Fei Jin[1]

[1] China Gridcom Co., Ltd., Shenzhen 518109, China
tangyuanyang@qq.com

[2] Shenzhen SmartChip Microelectronics Technology Co., Ltd., Shenzhen 518017, China

Abstract. Recently, load forecasting based on machine learning and artificial intelligence has shown great promise. As an individual with high power load, the accurate load forecasting of the special transformer users can guide the planning of future power generation and transmission, which is the key to ensuring the safe, stable and efficient running of the power system. However, most forecasting models do not consider the actual power consumption data of users and the power load characteristics of different types of users, and their application practicability and stability are insufficient. In this paper, we present a load forecasting syncretic model based on user unsupervised classification. Firstly, in the unsupervised classification of users, multiple features and similarities are introduced at the same time to realize the primary classification of special users. Secondly, with two time series clustering methods as the core, the secondary classification of special users is realized. Finally, different time series forecasting models are used for the power load curve characteristics of different user categories. Our model has achieved the best results in multiple metrics (RMSE: 0.359, MSE: 0129, MAE: 0.079, CR: 0.881), which can effectively improve the stability and accuracy of the load forecasting of the special transformer users.

Keywords: Special Transformer Users · Load Forecasting · Unsupervised Classification · Autoformer

1 Introduction

With the advancement of new power system construction [4] and the continuous development of market-oriented power production and consumption, the construction of new power systems faces numerous challenges and opportunities. In the context of new power systems, accurate load forecasting plays a crucial role. It not only aids power generation entities in formulating generation plans and scheduling maintenance but also assists grid operators in price determination and electricity dispatch, guiding user power consumption patterns and maintaining stable grid operations.

With the advancement of artificial intelligence, power load forecasting has become a crucial component in the operation and planning of power systems. Presently, there

Y. Yang et al. (Eds.): AIMS 2023, LNCS 14202, pp. 85–101, 2023.
https://doi.org/10.1007/978-3-031-45140-9_8

are five main approaches to load forecasting: econometric modeling, machine learning, deep learning, model ensemble, and cluster-based forecasting. Among these, econometric modeling methods [1, 12, 23, 26], exemplified by the ARIMA, forecast future sequence values based on the weak stationarity and differential properties of time series data. Machine learning methods [2, 16, 27, 29] utilize manual feature engineering and linear regression to forecast future sequence values. Deep learning methods [3, 15, 17, 20–22] utilize neural networks to automatically extract features for load forecasting. Model ensemble methods [7, 13, 18, 32] combine the characteristics of multiple time series forecasting models to enhance the accuracy of load forecasting. Cluster-based forecasting methods [8, 14, 24] use time series clustering results to forecast power loads for different clusters of users, reducing model training and inference cost. However, these methods do not fully consider the real-world power data and the load characteristics of different user categories, leading to limitations in practicality and stability. Additionally, the model construction methodologies of these methods could be further optimized, and there is room for improvement in accuracy.

To address the aforementioned issues, this paper initially preprocesses the power load data of special transformer users [5]. It introduces methods for handling missing values and outliers. Furthermore, an unsupervised user classification method is proposed, incorporating features like coefficient of variation [31], Hamming distance [25], DTW [19] and K-Shape [9] calculations to achieve primary and secondary user classifications. By leveraging power load curve characteristics, users are effectively divided into different categories, resolving the challenge posed by the complex and diverse power usage patterns among users and improving load forecasting stability. Subsequently, a multi-model fusion method is introduced, combining exponential smoothing, rule-based model, and the Autoformer. This approach adapt different forecasting models to different categories of special transformer users, selecting models based on the characteristics of power load curve data. This enhances load forecasting accuracy by adapting forecasting of the unique features of different power load patterns.

2 The Proposed Approach

This paper provides an approach for power load forecasting of special transformer users (see Fig. 1). The specific steps are as following:

(1) Designing Imputation and Outlier Handling Methods: Developing imputation method for missing values and method for handling outliers based on the characteristics of the collected real-world power load data, ensuring the usability of data.

(2) Unsupervised User Classification Model: Utilizing an unsupervised user classification model, involving two rounds of classification and clustering processes. This methodology divides a substantial number of special transformer users into distinct user categories based on power load characteristics.

(3) Load Forecasting Process: Building upon the unsupervised user classification results, during the load forecasting for a large number of users, the model training and load forecasting are executed solely for a single user category at a given time.

(4) Multi-model Fusion Approach: Following a multi-model fusion approach, distinct time series forecasting models are selected according to the power load characteristics of various user categories.

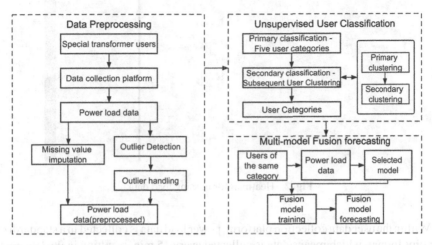

Fig. 1. Diagram of the load power forecasting technology of special transformer users

3   Data Preprocessing

In the power load forecasting of special transformer users, data preprocessing plays a crucial role throughout the entire process. It enhances the practicality of real-world data and directly influences the effectiveness of next tasks, including unsupervised user classification and multi-model fusion forecasting. This paper focuses on the preprocessing of special transformer users' power load data, which consists of two major modules: the missing value imputation module and the outlier handling module.

3.1   Missing Value Imputation

In the new power system, the consumption power load data of special transformer users are collected through a user data collection platform. In practical application scenarios, there is a probabilistic occurrence of data missing at various stages such as data collection, transmission, and storage. By performing statistical analysis on the collected data from all users, the overall missing rate of data is found to be 2.70%. The data missing situation is illustrated in Fig. 2. In this figure, the horizontal axis represents the date, the vertical axis represents special transformer users, and the heatmap value indicates the missing status of the 96-point data for a day. A value of 0 indicates all missing, while a value of 1 indicates no missing.

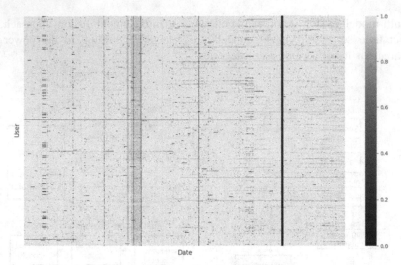

Fig. 2. Heatmap for missing load data

Within the user data collection platform, power load data is collected in a standardized 96-point format, which means data is collected every 15 min, resulting in 96 data points collected each day. In this data format, imputation of missing values in power load data involves two methods: direct linear interpolation method and daily linear interpolation method.

Direct Linear Interpolation. In the process of direct linear interpolation, missing data points in the power load data are directly filled using linear interpolation [28], resulting in imputed values that align with the data's inherent trend. This method utilizes a linear function, employing known data points before and after the missing data points to calculate a linear interpolation and fill these points.

Daily Linear Interpolation. During the process of daily linear interpolation, missing data points in the power load data are filled using linear interpolation on a daily basis. The imputed values obtained through this process align with the daily trend of the data. Specifically, a linear function is employed by utilizing known data points from the same position in the before and after days. This daily linear interpolation is used to fill in the missing data points at the same position.

3.2 Outlier Handling

Anomalies in power load data deviate from the normal power consumption patterns and may arise from abnormal events or behaviors, such as data collection errors, data entry mistakes, power outages, power theft, or irregular metering incidents. Anomalies stand out significantly from the other data points in terms of distribution, values, or periodic patterns. Anomalies in the power load data curve are illustrated in Fig. 3.

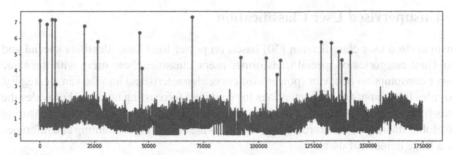

Fig. 3. The outliers of power load data

Sequence Sliding Window Detection. In sequence sliding window detection, the process involves sliding a window over the original sequence to detect outlier within each windowed subsequence. This process is performed iteratively, and the outliers from various windowed subsequences are combined eventually. The detection process is illustrated in Fig. 4.

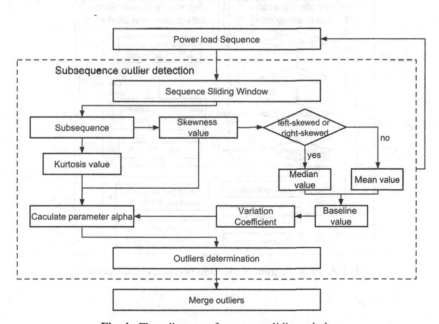

Fig. 4. Flow diagram of sequence sliding window

Handling of Outliers. After completing the detection of outlier in the whole sequence data, the outliers are covered by considering them as missing value using the missing value imputation method described above.

4   Unsupervised User Classification

Unsupervised user classification [30] based on power load data, identifies special and abnormal categories of special transformer users, classifies these users with the same power consumption behavior (power load curve characteristics) into the same category, provides label inputs of user categories for next load forecasting tasks, and provides the basis for power load forecasting model construction. Ultimately, on the basis of ensuring the global stability of load forecasting, it reduces the cost of model training and inference for a large number of users.

The unsupervised user classification contains two steps: primary classification, using the power load data as input, dividing the users into five user categories; secondary classification, based on the two-times clusters to achieve the clustering of annual periodic users and daily periodic users, and dividing users with the same seasonality and trends into the same type. The unsupervised user classification process is shown in Fig. 5.

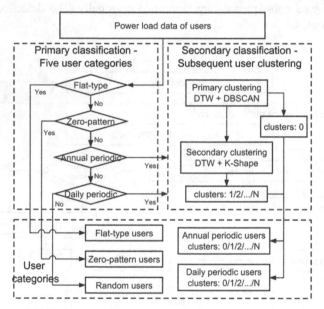

Fig. 5. Flow diagram of user unsupervised classification

4.1   Five User Categories

By analyzing the power consumption pattern and power load curve characteristics of a large number of special transformer users, users are set into five user categories.

Flat-Type Users. Classification is performed based on the power load sequence, which first determines whether the user is a flat-type or not. Flat-type users have basically the same power load value at any point in time, and the power load curve is basically maintained as a horizontal line.

Zero-Pattern Users. In the rest users, it is determined whether the user's power load sequence is a zero-pattern. Zero-pattern users only have power loads at certain times of the year and have very similar load curve profiles, such as agricultural users only use power at certain planting and harvesting period.

Annual Periodic Users. If it is not a zero-pattern user, then determine whether the user's power load sequence is an annual periodic. The power load curve of the annual periodic users takes the year as a cycle, and the power load curve on the same date in each year is very close, such as commercial users.

Daily Periodic Users. If the user is not a annual-periodic, then determine whether the user's power load sequence is daily-periodic. The load curve of daily-periodic users have a certain periodicity on a daily or weekly cycle. For example, factory users and so on.

Random Users. If the user's power load sequence does not satisfy any of these flat-type, zero-pattern, annual periodic and daily periodic, it means that the sequence does not match the established load curve characteristics, and therefore the user is judged to be a random user.

4.2 Subsequent User Clustering

After the above classification of the five user categories, there is still a problem of inconsistent power load curve characteristics for annual-periodic users and daily-periodic users. The power load curve characteristics of these users under the same category may differ greatly, and it is difficult to use a global model to achieve load forecasting for all users at the same time with a high accuracy rate. Therefore, a secondary classification, user clustering, is needed for the two categories of users, and the subsequent user clustering steps are as follows:

Step 1: Primary clustering. DBSCAN clustering model is performed based on the users, and a part of the anomalous user are obtained by density clustering, which are independent of other users' load curve and are clustering into cluster 0.

Step 2: Secondary clustering. Eliminate the samples with the cluster 0 from the users, and then perform the second K-Shape clustering. K-Shape clustering will be based on the power load curves of different users according to the similarity of curve shapes, and will clustering the same users of curve shape under the same cluster.

4.3 User Classification Results

After the above twice classification and twice clustering, unsupervised classification of a large number of special transformer users can be achieved. Using the numbers 1–5 to denote flat-type, zero-pattern, annual periodic, daily periodic and random, respectively, then the final classification result labels are shown in Table 1.

Table 1. Unsupervised user classification result labels

User Category	User Category Index	Labels
Flat-Type Users	1	C^1
Zero-Pattern Users	2	C^2
Annual Periodic Users	3	C_0^3
		C_1^3
		$\ldots\ldots$
		$C_{N.Class}^3$
Daily Periodic Users	4	C_0^4
		C_1^4
		$\ldots\ldots$
		$C_{N.Class}^4$
Random Users	5	C^5

5   Multi-Model Fusion Forecasting

After the aforementioned unsupervised user classification, a large number of special transformer users are assigned to user categories. Within each user category, the users exhibit similar load curve characteristics. Therefore, it is necessary to select different forecasting models that cater to the distinct load curve characteristics.

5.1   Flat-Type Users

Flat-Type Users, whose power load remains relatively constant at any given time point. Intuitively, this means that the load curve does not significantly change over time and remains essentially a flat line. From an objective perspective, this can be understood as a weak stationarity property of the time series, where any time interval of the load curve exhibits a similar autocovariance [34], indicating time invariance of the autocovariance with respect to time shifts.

Based on the characteristics of the power load curve for flat-type users, the exponential smoothing is chosen as the load forecasting model.

Exponential Smoothing. Exponential smoothing is a model where the smoothed value for any given period is a weighted sum of the current observed value and the previous smoothed value. Exponential smoothing assigns different weights to observations at different points in time, giving higher weight to newer observations and lower weight to older observations. This allows the latest trends to be quickly reflected in the exponential smoothing forecasting. Exponential smoothing model includes single exponential smoothing, double exponential smoothing, and triple exponential smoothing [33].

Single Exponential Smoothing. In single exponential smoothing, the forecast value for the next period is equal to a weighted sum of the current actual value and the current forecast value. This method is suitable for time series forecasting with no significant trends or seasonality.

Double Exponential Smoothing. Double exponential smoothing is a further smoothing of the single exponential smoothing method and is suitable for time series forecasting with a linear trend and no seasonality.

Triple Exponential Smoothing. Triple exponential smoothing is a further smoothing of the double exponential smoothing method and is suitable for time series forecasting with trends and seasonality.

Flat-Type Load Forecasting. Due to the fact that the power load curve for flat-type users remains essentially a flat line without significant trends or seasonality, the single exponential smoothing method is chosen as the power load forecasting model for flat-type users.

5.2 Zero-Pattern Users

Zero-Pattern Users, also known as intermittent users, exhibit power load during certain periods of the year, with a consistent power load pattern that closely repeats annually. However, their power load values are zero for the remaining time. Based on the characteristics of the power load curve for zero-pattern users, a combination of single exponential smoothing forecasting in annual periodicity and triple exponential smoothing forecasting in daily periodicity is chosen. The two forecasting results are weighted and summed to obtain the final power load forecasting result.

5.3 Annual Periodic Users

Annual periodic users are characterized by power load curves that follow an annual periodicity, with the curve characteristics on the same date in each year being very similar. After segmenting users into this category, they can be further divided into subcategories. Within the same subcategory, the power load curves exhibit similar trends and seasonality, while still adhering to the annual periodicity. Therefore, by using a single global power load forecasting model for the users within the same subcategory, both the stability of power load forecasting and the reduction of training and inference costs can be ensured.

Autoformer Model. Based on the characteristics of the power load curve of annual periodic users, the Autoformer time series forecasting model [10] is chosen. Autoformer is a long sequence forecasting model based on deep factorization architecture and autocorrelation mechanism. The reasons for selecting this model are as follows:

(1) It can take data of multiple users within the same subcategory as model inputs simultaneously, resulting in a single global model, thereby reducing the training and inference costs.
(2) When data of multiple users are trained together, the model can learn the trend and seasonality information of each user's power load data separately.

(3) It can convert information such as date into static features to be used as inputs for model training and inference.

Annual Periodic Load Forecasting. The specific steps for conducting load forecasting for annual periodic users are as follows:

(1) The power load data for users labeled as subcategory C_0^3 is converted into matrix format $X_{u,k}$ where u represents users and k represents the power load curve.
(2) The power load data $X_{u,k}$ is transformed into the input format of Autoformer, and multiple user data are simultaneously used as inputs for model training, resulting in the power load forecasting global model $Model_0^3$.
(3) Using the model $Model_0^3$ simultaneous power load forecasting inference is performed for all users labeled as C_0^3 resulting in the forecast value for users within the specific subcategory.
(4) The user data with the subcategory label C_1^3, C_2^3, ..., $C_{N.Class}^3$ for annual periodic users are individually processed through steps 1) to 3), resulting in forecast power load results for users within each specific subcategory.

5.4 Daily Periodic Users

Daily Periodic Users are characterized by power load curves that follow a daily (or weekly) periodicity, with very similar power load curve characteristics on each day (or week). After segmenting daily periodic users continuously, we obtain different subcategories. Within the same subcategory, the power load curves of users exhibit similar trends and seasonality while adhering to the daily (or weekly) periodic pattern. Therefore, using a single global power load forecasting model for the users within the same subcategory can ensure power load forecasting stability while reducing the training and inference costs.

For power load forecasting of daily periodic users, the same long time series forecasting model, Autoformer, is chosen. The reasons for this selection and the specific steps are the same as those for annual periodic users.

5.5 Random Users

Random users are characterized by power load curves that do not exhibit clear trends or periodic patterns. Therefore, the neural network model Autoformer, which has stronger capabilities in feature extraction and representation, is chosen. Autoformer has shown the best performance in long sequence forecasting task.

6 Experimental Analysis

6.1 Overview of Dataset

The selected dataset consists of power load data for 1,677 special transformer users from an power province company. The time range covers five years from January 1, 2017, to December 31, 2021, with a time resolution of 15 min. The dataset is divided into a training set (from January 1, 2017 to December 31, 2020) and a test set (from January 1, 2021 to December 31, 2021) based on the time dimension. The dataset then undergoes data preprocessing, unsupervised user classification, multi-model fusion forecasting, and analysis of experimental results in sequence.

6.2 Unsupervised User Classification

After data preprocessing and performing unsupervised user classification on all 1,677 special transformer users, we obtained the following classification results: 189 users classified as Flat-Type Users, 65 users classified as Zero-Pattern Users, 492 users classified as Annual Periodic Users, 751 users classified as Daily Periodic Users and 180 users classified as Random Users. One user was selected from each of the five user categories, and the power load data for these users were visualized and analyzed. The results align with the predefined characteristics of power load curves, as shown in Fig. 6.

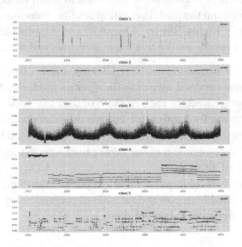

Fig. 6. Load curves for five user categories

The Annual Periodic Users were further categorized, resulting in user classification labels $C_0^3, C_1^3, C_2^3, \ldots\ldots, C_{N.Class}^3$. Similarly, the Daily Periodic Users were categorized, resulting in user classification labels $C_0^4, C_1^4, C_2^4, \ldots\ldots, C_{N.Class}^4$. For the results of user subcategorization, the power load data was visualized and analyzed in terms of curves. The analysis demonstrated that users within the same subcategory exhibit similar power load curve characteristics, including similar trends and seasonality patterns, as shown in Fig. 7.

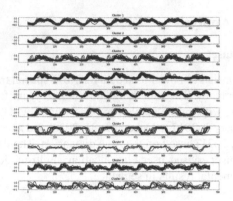

Fig. 7. Load curves for different user categories

6.3 Multi-Model Fusion Forecasting

Evaluation Metrics. In this paper, the evaluation for power load forecasting are assessed using four metrics: mean absolute error (MAE), mean squared error (MSE), root mean squared error (RMSE), and accuracy (C_R [11]).

Experimental Results Comparison. After completing the data preprocessing, the proposed unsupervised user classification method and multi-model fusion forecasting method are utilized to obtain the load forecasting results. Subsequently, the comparison analysis models, namely LightGBM [6], DeepAR, and Autoformer, are used to obtain power load forecasting results for the five user categories and the entire users.

Data Preprocessing and Unsupervised User Classification. Based on the data preprocessing method and unsupervised user classification method, the Autoformer model is used to forecast the power load for each of the five user categories. The RMSE is then calculated, considering the forecasting for all five user categories together. As a comparison group for unsupervised user classification, the power load is directly forecasted for the entire users. The comparison of the power load forecasting results can be found in the row information of Table 2.

Meanwhile, the last two columns of Table 2 represent the comparison between load forecasting results obtained from power data without preprocessing and load forecasting results obtained from preprocessed power data.

Table 2. Supervised vs. Unsupervised classification

User Category		Autoformer (RMSE)	
		Data Without Preprocessing	Data With Preprocessing
Unsupervised User Classification	Flat-Type	0.361	0.359
	Zero-Pattern	0.643	0.642
	Annual Periodic	0.380	0.377
	Daily Periodic	0.313	0.305
	Random	0.442	0.442
	Overall Result	0.371	0.367
Entire Users	–	0.421	0.416

Analysis of the results in the above table reveals the following conclusions:

(1) Data preprocessing methods can improve the effectiveness of load forecasting results and enhance the practicality of real-world data from special transformer users.
(2) The unsupervised user classification method, which divides users with similar trends and periodic patterns into groups before performing load forecasting, can enhance the stability of subsequent forecasting task.

Multi-Model Fusion Forecasting. Based on the multi-model fusion forecasting method, incorporating the aforementioned data preprocessing and unsupervised user classification results, load forecasting is performed using the LightGBM, DeepAR, and Autoformer models. The results are compared with the multi-model fusion forecasting method proposed in this paper. The comparison of evaluation metrics for load forecasting of the five user categories is presented in Table 3, while the comparison of evaluation metrics for overall results is shown in Table 4.

Analysing the comparison of the evaluation metrics in Table 3, it can be seen that the multi-model fusion forecasting method proposed in this paper generally outperforms the comparison model in the forecast results of the five user categories.

By calculating the comprehensive evaluation metrics for the five user categories from Table 3, we obtain a comparison of the evaluation metrics for the overall results in Table 4. It can be observed that using the multi-model fusion forecasting method proposed in this paper yields better results than the comparison model in all evaluation metrics. Specifically, the four evaluation metrics show improvements of at least 2.23%, 4.65%, 11.39%, and 0.8%, respectively.

Table 3. Comparison of different models for five categories

Metric	Model				
	User Category	LightGBM	DeepAR	Autoformer	Proposed
RMSE	flag-type	0.456	0.375	**0.359**	0.369
	zero-pattern	0.736	0.704	0.642	**0.574**
	annual periodic	0.395	0.382	0.377	**0.374**
	daily periodic	0.310	0.309	0.305	**0.293**
	random	0.508	0.496	0.442	**0.442**
MSE	flag-type	0.208	0.175	**0.129**	0.136
	zero-pattern	0.541	0.511	0.412	**0.330**
	annual periodic	0.156	0.151	0.142	**0.140**
	daily periodic	0.096	0.095	0.093	**0.086**
	random	0.258	0.213	0.195	**0.195**
MAE	flag-type	0.116	0.097	0.068	**0.047**
	zero-pattern	0.340	0.313	0.258	**0.180**
	annual periodic	0.099	**0.091**	0.099	0.098
	daily periodic	**0.052**	0.058	0.062	0.055
	random	0.159	0.133	0.124	**0.124**
C_R	flag-type	0.855	0.801	0.570	**0.896**
	zero-pattern	0.735	0.753	0.765	**0.823**
	annual periodic	0.882	0.882	0.884	**0.885**
	daily periodic	**0.901**	0.894	0.874	0.886
	random	0.849	0.859	0.864	**0.864**

Table 4. Comparison of different models for total users

Metric	Model			
	LightGBM	DeepAR	Autoformer	Proposed
RMSE	0.401	0.383	0.367	**0.359**
MSE	0.161	0.149	0.135	**0.129**
MAE	0.096	0.090	0.088	**0.079**
C_R	0.873	0.866	0.810	**0.881**

7 Conclusion

This paper introduces a power load forecasting approach specifically tailored for special transformer users. Firstly, a data preprocessing method is proposed to solve the missing value and outliers in the real-world datasets.

Secondly, an unsupervised user classification approach is proposed, consisting of five user categories method and subsequent user clustering method. Users with similar power load curve characteristics are grouped into the same category, forming the foundation for dataset partitioning in subsequent load forecasting task, effectively improving result stability.

Next, a multi-model fusion forecasting approach is presented. By combining distinct time series forecasting model and considering the power load curve attributes of different user categories, this method employs various models for load forecasting, including exponential smoothing, rule-based models, and the Autoformer. This strategy enhances forecast accuracy significantly.

Lastly, experimental validation is performed using real power load data from an power province company. Through comparative analysis of experimental results, the following conclusions are drawn:

- The proposed data preprocessing approach effectively addresses missing value and outlier issues in special transformer users. It ensures accuracy in subsequent tasks and strengthens the usability of real-world data.
- The introduced unsupervised user classification approach effectively groups users with similar power load curve characteristics, forming the basis for dataset partitioning in power load forecasting task. This effectively enhances forecast result stability.
- The multi-model fusion forecasting approach, combining different time series forecasting models, tailored to power load curve characteristics of users, which significantly improves forecast accuracy.
- By combining the unsupervised user classification and multi-model fusion forecasting, a single global power load forecasting model is used for users within the same subcategory. This approach, while ensuring stable and accurate load forecasting results, substantially reduces model training and inference costs.

References

1. Sun, Y., Wang, Y., Zhu, W., Li, Y.: Residential daily power load forecasting based on threshold ARMA model considering the influence of temperature. Electr. Power Constr. 43(09), 117–124 (2022)
2. Liu, J., Zhao, J., Feng, Y., Zhou, C., Jiang, M., Zhang, H.: Power load forecasting in power internet of things based on gradient boosting decision tree. Smart Power 50(08), 46–53 (2022)
3. Yao, G., Li, T., Liu, L., Zheng, Y.: Residential electricity load forecasting method based on DAE and LSTM. Control Eng. China 29(11), 2048–2053 (2022)
4. Liu, Y., Ma, Q., Wang, Z., Li, P., Liu, C.: Cogitation on power and electricity balance dispatching in new power system. Proc. CSEE 43(05), 1694–1706 (2023)

5. Cheng, J., Xie, F., Han, S.-C., Lu, X., Lv, L.: Design of customer real-name information collection and storage model for power marketing system. Tech. Autom. Appl. **41**(04), 38–41+62 (2022)
6. Xu, Y., Zhang, X., Zhou, X., Sun, J., Qiu, X., Xie, L.: The short-term load forecasting method for transformer based on prophet-LightGBM. J. North China Electr. Power Univ. (Nat. Sci. Ed.) **12**(29), 1–7 (2022)
7. Dat, N.Q., Ngoc Anh, N.T., Nhat Anh, N., et al.: Hybrid online model based multi seasonal decompose for short-term electricity load forecasting using ARIMA and online RNN. J. Intell. Fuzzy Syst. **41**(5), 5639–5652 (2021)
8. Wang, Z., et al.: Electric bus charging load forecasting method based on spectral clustering and LSTM neural network. Electr. Power Constr. **58**(06), 58–66 (2021)
9. Li, H., Jia, R., Tan, G.: Fuzzy classification for time series on K-Shape. J. Univ. Electron. Sci. Technol. China **50**(06), 899–906 (2021)
10. Wu, H., Xu, J., Wang, J., et al.: Autoformer: decomposition transformers with auto-correlation for long-term series forecasting. Adv. Neural Inf. Process. Syst. **34**, 22419–22430 (2021)
11. China State Administration for Market Supervision and Regulation, China National Standardisation Administration. GB/T 40607-2021 Technical requirements for dispatching side forecasting system of wind or photovoltaic power. Beijing: Standards Press of China, 2021
12. Guantong, H., Lanxin, H.: Short-term load forecasting model based on EEMD-LSTS-ARIMA. J. Phys. Conf. Ser. **1684**(1), 012045 (2020). IOP Publishing
13. Zhenyu, C., et al.: Ultra short-term power load forecasting based on combined LSTM-XGBoost model. Power Syst. Technol. **44**(02), 614–620 (2020)
14. Xie, M., Chai, C., Guo, H., Wang, M.: Household electricity load forecasting based on pearson correlation coefficient clustering and convolutional neural network. In: Proceedings of 2020 4th International Conference on Electrical, Mechanical and Computer Engineering (ICEMCE 2020), vol. 1 (2020)
15. Deng, Z., Wang, B., Guo, H., et al.: Unified quantile regression deep neural network with time-cognition for probabilistic residential load forecasting. Complexity **2020**, 1–18 (2020)
16. Chen, M., Liu, Q., Chen, S., et al.: XGBoost-based algorithm interpretation and application on post-fault transient stability status prediction of power system. IEEE Access **7**, 13149–13158 (2019)
17. Bao, W.-Q., Chen, J., Xiong, T.: Research on short-term power load forecasting based on evolving neural network. Electr. Eng. (11), 46–49 (2019)
18. Ju, Y., Sun, G., Chen, Q., et al.: A model combining convolutional neural network and Light-GBM algorithm for ultra-short-term wind power forecasting. IEEE Access **7**, 28309–28318 (2019)
19. Meiying, Q., Yuxiang, L., Hui, T.: A similarity metric algorithm for multivariate based on information entropy and DTW. Acta Sci. Natur. Univ. Sunyatseni **58**(02), 1–8 (2019)
20. Zhuo, C., Longxiang, S.: Short-term electrical load forecasting based on deep learning LSTM network. Electron. Technol. **47**(01), 39–41 (2018)
21. Shi, H., Xu, M., Li, R.: Deep learning for household load forecasting—a novel pooling deep RNN. IEEE Trans. Smart Grid **9**(5), 5271–5280 (2017)
22. Kumar, J., Goomer, R., Singh, A.K.: Long short term memory recurrent neural network (LSTM-RNN) based workload forecasting model for cloud datacenters. Procedia Comput. Sci. **125**, 676–682 (2018)
23. Tan, F., Zhang, Z., Zhu, C., Zhang, J.: Optimized exponential smoothing foe load forecast. Power Demand Side Manag. **18**(06), 22–26 (2016)
24. Al-Otaibi, R., Jin, N., Wilcox, T., et al.: Feature construction and calibration for clustering daily load curves from smart-meter data. IEEE Trans. Ind. Inform. **12**(2), 645–654 (2016)

25. Computer Science Research; Studies from University of Padua Update Current Data on Computer Science Research (Sequence similarity measures based on bounded hamming distance). Computer Weekly News, 2016: 359
26. Cui, H., Peng, X.: Summer short-term load forecasting based on ARIMAX model. Power Syst. Prot. Control **43**(04), 108–114 (2015)
27. Wang, X., Meng, L.: Ultra-short-term load forecasting based on EEMD-LSSVM. Power Syst. Prot. Control **43**(1), 61–65 (2015)
28. Yu, Y., Mu, Y.: Research on interpolation algorithm. Mod. Comput. **1**(05), 32–35 (2014)
29. Wei, R.R., Wei, Z.Z., Rong, R., et al.: Short term load forecasting based on PCA and LS-SVM. Adv. Mater. Res. **756**, 4193–4197 (2013)
30. Bandyopadhyay, S., Saha, S.: Unsupervised Classification: Similarity Measures, Classical and Metaheuristic Approaches, and Applications. Springer, Berlin, Heidelberg (2013). https://doi.org/10.1007/978-3-642-32451-2
31. Wang, W.: Coefficient of variation - a simple and useful statistical indicator to measure the degree of dispersion. China Stati. **306**(06), 41–42 (2007)
32. Chen, Y., Wang, L., Long, H.: Short-term load forecasting with model neural network. Proc. CSEE **04**(18), 79–82 (2001)
33. Xu, D.: A further study on the exponential smoothing estimation method for parameters of forecasting model and its application. Syst. Eng. Theory Pract. **19**(2), 25–30 (1999)
34. McLeod, I.: Derivation of the theoretical autocovariance function of autoregressive-moving average time series. Appl. Stat. **24**(2), 255–256 (1975)

Edge AI Patterns

Richard Shan[1][✉] and Tony Shan[2]

[1] Computing Technology Solutions Inc., Charlotte, USA
m@richardshan.com
[2] Charlotte, NC 28277, USA

Abstract. This paper comprehensively explores a spectrum of AI patterns tailored for edge computing, including regular, branched, circular, serial, concurrent, cascade, input fusion, hierarchical, and ensemble patterns. As edge devices grapple with limited resources and the need for real-time decision-making, these patterns offer structured methodologies for efficient data processing, adaptive decision-making, and enhanced accuracy. Through in-depth analyses of each pattern's characteristics, approaches, and implementations, the pattern model equips users with a systematic understanding of the diverse strategies available for orchestrating AI workflows in edge computing environments, paving the way for improved system design, scalability, and performance across a myriad of application domains.

Keywords: Pattern · AI · edge computing · edge AI · classification · single task · multiple tasks · mixed run · regular · branched · circular · serial · concurrent · cascade · input fusion · hierarchical · ensemble

1 Introduction

In today's hyper-connected world, the rapid proliferation of Internet of Things (IoT) devices, 5G networks, and cloud computing has brought about an unprecedented surge in data generation and consumption. As traditional centralized computing architectures struggle to keep pace with the deluge of data, a revolutionary paradigm has emerged to address the challenges of latency, bandwidth, and security – Edge Computing. The concept of Edge Computing marks a pivotal shift in how we process and analyze data, moving computation closer to the source of data generation, and redefining the landscape of modern computing.

Edge Computing represents an ingenious solution that redistributes computational tasks from a centralized cloud infrastructure to the "edge" of the network, where data is produced and consumed. By leveraging a decentralized network of edge nodes, comprising smart devices, gateways, and micro-data centers, Edge Computing optimizes data processing, storage, and analytics in close proximity to the data's origin. This approach not only minimizes the inherent drawbacks of latency and bandwidth bottlenecks but also empowers industries and individuals with real-time insights and actionable intelligence.

While edge computing holds the potential to transform the landscape of distributed computing, several significant barriers and obstacles hinder its widespread adoption and

Y. Yang et al. (Eds.): AIMS 2023, LNCS 14202, pp. 102–116, 2023.
https://doi.org/10.1007/978-3-031-45140-9_9

implementation. The key headaches and constraints in edge computing include heterogeneous infrastructure, limited resources, data management and distribution, scalability and load balancing, security and privacy concerns, interoperability and standards, network connectivity and reliability, edge node management and maintenance, and regulatory and legal considerations. These challenges arise due to the unique characteristics of edge computing environments, which involve distributed nodes, varied resources, and real-time data processing. Understanding these barriers is essential to address them effectively and realize the full potential of edge computing.

As edge computing continues to evolve, it becomes further imperative to confront the challenges that arise in order to fully exploit its capabilities. Ding et al. articulated a Dagstuhl perspective, outlining the roadmap for edge AI [1]. Tziouvaras and Foukalas expounded upon three distinct Edge AI techniques tailored for industrial IoT scenarios [2]. Wu et al. presented a novel Edge-AI-driven framework, seamlessly integrating efficient mobile network design with facial expression recognition. This architecture utilizes an edge-cloud joint inference model to achieve low-latency inferences [3]. Raith et al. proposed a comprehensive framework facilitating the definition, execution, and analysis of distributed load testing experiments for benchmarking edge-cloud clusters [4]. In a related context, Le et al. introduced BrainyEdge, an AI-enabled framework designed specifically for IoT edge computing [5]. Additionally, Narayanan et al. put forth a pioneering approach that fuses pipeline-parallel training with traditional intra-batch parallelism, accelerating system convergence [6].

Tackling complex barriers and obstacles requires innovative solutions. One such approach is the utilization of patterns, or best practices, that offer standardized and proven solutions to common challenges faced in edge computing. Implementing well-designed patterns can enhance the scalability, efficiency, security, and resilience of edge computing systems, thus enabling the realization of their full potential across various domains. In our view, it is imperative to take a pattern approach for edge computing due to the immaturity, complication, inconsistency, fragmentation, and compliance in this domain. To the best of our knowledge, no published work exists today that comprehensively classifies and analyzes edge patterns with in-depth evaluations of strengths, weaknesses, applicability, and best practices.

We will delve into a pattern model in the next section. Section 3 to 5 will cover individual patterns in the Edge AI space. Section 6 provides the best practices of applying these patterns, followed by the conclusion in Sect. 7.

2 Pattern Model

In the past few decades, a plethora of patterns has emerged across various fields. These range from the seminal 23 design patterns introduced by the Gang of Four [7] to patterns encompassing technology strategies [8], cloud-native methodologies [9], and even Kubernetes deployment [10]. While some of these existing patterns can be directly applied to edge computing with minimal adaptations, others can be combined and repurposed to be indirectly employed in the context of edge. Certain patterns may necessitate substantial revisions to suit the unique demands of edge computing.

Moreover, certain patterns can be extrapolated or enhanced by existing ones to tailor methods specifically to fit edge requirements. Entirely novel patterns have been devised to address the distinctive challenges that arise in the realm of edge computing. To systematically organize this diverse array of patterns, we introduce a comprehensive pattern model categorized into modules: AI, Composite, Clustering, Edge-native, Sense-response, and Segmentation (referred to as ACCESS).

The AI module in ACCESS consists of the Edge AI patterns, which are a set of reusable solution designs and guidelines that describe how to implement AI applications on edge devices. These patterns can help improve the performance, latency, security, and flexibility of AI applications in edge computing. AI patterns improve performance by processing data locally on edge devices, reducing latency and improving responsiveness of AI applications, and enhance security by processing data closer to the source, making it difficult for attackers to access sensitive data. AI patterns increase flexibility by allowing applications to be deployed closer to end users, improving the performance and responsiveness of AI applications.

We further itemize the patterns in the AI module, as illustrated in Fig. 1.

- Single Task: Regular, Branched, and Circular
- Multiple Tasks: Serial, Concurrent, and Cascade
- Mixed Run: Input Fusion, Hierarchical, and Ensemble

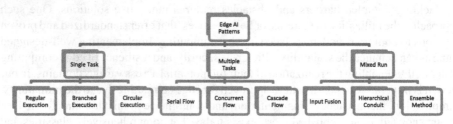

Fig. 1. Edge AI Pattern Structure

The documentation of a technology pattern should provide a high-level overview of the pattern, including its purpose, benefits, and limitations. The documentation should also be clear and concise, so that it can be easily understood by a wide range of audiences. To make it consistent, we use a standardized format to document patterns: Realization, Example, Description, Approach, and Name (REDAN).

- Name: a term by which a pattern is designated and distinguished from others
- Description: an overview of a pattern and intended use
- Approach: the techniques to apply a pattern to solve a problem
- Realization: the tools and steps involved to implement a pattern
- Example: a specific use case or case study of a pattern

3 Single Task

3.1 Regular Execution

Description
The Regular Execution pattern involves deploying AI models and algorithms directly on edge devices or edge servers, enabling real-time data processing, analysis, and decision-making at the network's edge. Instead of sending all data to a centralized cloud for processing, edge computing leverages local computational resources to perform AI tasks, reducing latency, bandwidth usage, and ensuring timely responses in latency-sensitive applications.

Approach
The approach of the Regular Execution pattern in edge computing requires specialized software and hardware components. AI models must be optimized for edge deployment, with consideration given to the unique resource constraints of edge devices. Techniques like model quantization, pruning, and utilization of lightweight architectures are essential to achieve efficient AI processing on the edge. Edge computing platforms and frameworks facilitate the deployment and management of AI models at the edge. These platforms provide the necessary runtime environments, libraries, and interfaces for edge AI execution. The selection of appropriate edge devices or edge servers is crucial for the successful implementation of edge AI. Devices with sufficient computational power, memory, and energy efficiency are preferred.

Realization
The implementation of the Regular Execution pattern consists of the following steps:

- Data Collection: Edge devices capture data from various sensors or devices in their proximity. This data can include sensor readings, video streams, audio recordings, or any other form of sensory input.
- Data Preprocessing: The raw data collected at the edge may need preprocessing before feeding it into AI models. Preprocessing involves data cleaning, feature extraction, normalization, or any other data transformation necessary to make it suitable for AI analysis.
- Inference at the Edge: AI models are deployed on the edge devices or edge servers to perform real-time inference on preprocessed data. Inference involves using the AI model to predict, classify, or make decisions based on the input data.
- Local Decision-Making: The model's output is used for local decision-making at the edge, without the need to send data to the central cloud. This localized decision-making enables rapid responses and reduces dependency on cloud connectivity.
- Data Aggregation (Optional): In certain cases, the edge devices may aggregate processed data and send it to the central cloud for further analysis or to train centralized AI models for better accuracy and insights.

Example
A smart traffic light system demonstrates an effective use of the Regular Execution pattern. In this system, cameras collect data on traffic flow. This data is then processed locally on edge devices to detect traffic congestion via an AI model. If the traffic is

determined to be congested, the edge devices can send a message to a controller to request that the traffic lights be adjusted. Once confirmed, the system then adjusts the traffic lights to improve traffic flow.

3.2 Branched Execution

Description
The Branched Execution pattern involves making decisions and branching out the execution of AI tasks based on specific conditions or criteria. This pattern enables dynamic adaptation of AI workflows, allowing different sequences of tasks to be executed depending on the outcomes of intermediate steps. Branched Execution is well-suited for scenarios where diverse actions are required based on varying data conditions or specific events.

Approach
The Branched Execution pattern approach involves evaluating conditions or triggers at different points in the AI workflow. Based on these conditions, the flow splits into different branches, each leading to a unique sequence of AI tasks. This approach requires decision-making logic to determine the appropriate path to follow, depending on the situation.

Realization
The implementation of the Branched Execution pattern has the following key aspects:

- Data Ingestion: Raw data is collected from IoT devices and ingested into the edge server using communication protocols like MQTT, CoAP, or HTTP.
- Data Preprocessing: The incoming data is preprocessed to clean, transform, and normalize it using libraries such as Pandas, NumPy, or scikit-learn.
- Condition Evaluation: Based on specific conditions, triggers, or rules, a decision is made to determine which path the flow should take. This condition can be evaluated using programming constructs or AI model outputs.
- Branched AI Tasks: Depending on the condition, the flow branches into different paths, each involving a sequence of AI tasks tailored to the specific condition. These tasks can include model inference, analytics, or data transformations.
- Result Aggregation and Post-Processing: The outputs from different branches are aggregated, and post-processing steps are performed to generate the final result or action. Post-processing may involve combining predictions or generating alerts.

Example
In an edge-enabled smart agriculture system, IoT sensors monitor soil moisture levels in different fields. An AI system then determines whether irrigation is required based on the collected data. Soil moisture data is collected from IoT sensors and sent to the edge server using MQTT. Raw soil moisture readings are normalized and transformed into meaningful moisture percentages. A decision is made to evaluate if irrigation is required. The condition might be a moisture threshold, along with the prediction from a rain forecast ML model.

In this example, the Branched Execution pattern is used to determine whether irrigation is needed based on soil moisture levels. Depending on the moisture condition, the flow either branches into irrigation actions or concludes without any action. This dynamic decision-making approach optimizes water usage in agriculture and showcases how AI flows can adapt to changing conditions at the edge.

3.3 Circular Execution

Description
The Circular Execution pattern involves the repetitive execution of a set of AI tasks within a loop or circular structure. This pattern is used when AI tasks need to be performed iteratively or when constant monitoring and analysis is required to adapt to changing conditions. The loop structure allows AI systems to continuously process data, update models, and make decisions in real-time.

Approach
In the Circular Execution pattern, the approach revolves around setting up a loop structure that iterates through a sequence of AI tasks. The loop can be based on a fixed number of iterations, predefined conditions, or continuous monitoring of data. The pattern's design ensures that the AI tasks are executed repeatedly, facilitating real-time updates and adjustments.

Realization
The implementation of the Circular Execution pattern includes the following key aspects:

- Data Preprocessing: The incoming data is preprocessed to prepare it for AI analysis, including cleaning, transformation, and normalization using libraries like Pandas, NumPy, or scikit-learn.
- Loop Initialization: The loop is initiated, setting up the conditions for the iterative execution of AI tasks.
- AI Tasks Execution: Within each iteration of the loop, AI tasks such as model inference, data analytics, or decision-making are performed based on the current data.
- Loop Condition Evaluation: After each iteration, the condition for loop continuation is evaluated. This condition might involve checking convergence, reaching a specific time threshold, or monitoring certain data attributes.
- Iteration Control: If the loop condition is met, the loop continues to the next iteration. If not, the loop terminates, and the final results or actions are generated.

Example
In an industrial IoT setting, machinery health is monitored using sensors. Predictive maintenance techniques are applied to determine maintenance needs and avoid unplanned downtime. Sensor data is collected from industrial machines and sent to the edge server using MQTT. Raw sensor readings are preprocessed to extract relevant features and normalize values. The loop is initiated to continuously monitor machine health and predict maintenance needs. AI models analyze sensor data to predict potential failures or maintenance requirements. Data analytics are performed to identify trends or anomalies. Decisions are made based on AI model outputs and data analysis results.

In this example, the Circular Execution pattern is employed to enable predictive maintenance. By continuously monitoring machine health and analyzing sensor data within a loop structure, the AI system can proactively detect potential failures and initiate maintenance actions before they escalate into unplanned downtime. This pattern exemplifies how AI flows can be adapted for real-time decision-making and continuous adaptation in edge computing environments.

4 Multiple Tasks

4.1 Serial Flow

Description
The Serial Flow pattern involves a sequential and linear execution of multiple artificial intelligence (AI) tasks on edge devices or edge servers. In this pattern, each AI task is performed one after the other, where each AI model is processed independently of the others. The pattern is characterized by its straightforward and deterministic nature, making it suitable for applications where a predefined sequence of AI operations is required.

Approach
The Serial Flow pattern is employed in edge computing environments for sequential analysis. The AI tasks need to be performed in a specific order to achieve the desired results. For instance, in natural language processing, tasks like text tokenization, part-of-speech tagging, and sentiment analysis need to be executed sequentially to provide meaningful insights. The dependency between tasks may also require the output of one AI task prior to the kickoff of next task, and subsequent tasks may rely on the information derived from the previous steps. In addition, edge devices may have limited computational resources, making parallel processing impractical. In such cases, executing tasks in a serial manner allows for efficient resource utilization to accommodate the constraints.

Realization
The implementation of the Serial Flow pattern consists of the following steps:

- Data Ingestion: The first step in the Serial AI Flow pattern is data ingestion, where raw data is collected from IoT devices or sensors. Tools like MQTT, CoAP, or HTTP can be used for efficient and lightweight data communication between edge devices and the edge server.
- Data Preprocessing: After data ingestion, the raw data is preprocessed to clean, normalize, and transform it into a format suitable for AI analysis. Python libraries like NumPy, Pandas, and scikit-learn are commonly used for data preprocessing tasks.
- AI Model Inference in Sequence: The next step involves AI model inference, where the preprocessed data is sequentially fed into multiple trained machine learning or deep learning models. Libraries like TensorFlow, PyTorch, or Keras can be used to deploy and execute AI models on edge devices.
- Post-Processing and Decision Making: Once the AI models produce predictions or insights, post-processing is performed to interpret the results and make decisions based on predefined rules or thresholds.

Example
In a smart retail scenario, a customer walks into a retail store and picks up a shirt to try, triggering AI models to be executed in a sequential order. The first model detects the shirt and identifies its style and material via a pre-trained model, such as YOLOv4. The second model predicts the price of the shirt based on its fabric, color, and other factors, using a machine learning model similar to linear regression. The third model recommends similar shirts to the customer based on their past purchase history and the store inventory.

4.2 Concurrent Flow

Description
The Concurrent Flow pattern involves the simultaneous execution of multiple AI tasks on edge devices or edge servers. Unlike the Serial Flow pattern, where tasks are executed sequentially, the Concurrent Flow pattern leverages the capabilities of multiple processing units to perform independent AI tasks concurrently. This pattern is employed to maximize resource utilization, reduce processing time, and achieve higher throughput in edge computing environments.

Approach
The Concurrent Flow pattern utilizes parallelism to divide AI tasks into independent sub-tasks, which are then distributed across available processing units. Each processing unit executes its assigned sub-task independently, in parallel with other units, enabling efficient utilization of computational resources.

Realization
The implementation of the Concurrent Flow pattern has the following key aspects:

- Data Ingestion: Raw data is collected from IoT devices or sensors and ingested into the edge server using communication protocols like MQTT, CoAP, or HTTP.
- Parallel Data Preprocessing: The raw data is divided into multiple batches, and each batch is independently preprocessed by separate processing units. Parallel data preprocessing is implemented using parallel processing libraries in programming languages such as Python's multiprocessing module.
- AI Model Parallelism: To perform AI model inference in parallel, the AI model is replicated, and each replica processes a separate batch of preprocessed data. Frameworks like TensorFlow's distributed training or model parallelism in PyTorch facilitate AI model parallelization.
- Aggregation and Post-Processing: The outputs from different AI model replicas are aggregated and combined to produce a unified result. Post-processing may involve further filtering or merging to generate the final output.

Example
In a smart city surveillance system, numerous cameras are deployed to monitor various areas. Object detection is performed in real-time to identify and track objects of interest, such as vehicles, pedestrians, or suspicious peoples. Video streams from surveillance cameras are sent to the edge server using MQTT or other communication protocols. The

incoming video streams are split into multiple segments, and each segment is independently preprocessed for noise reduction and frame extraction. The Python multiprocessing module is used to parallelize data preprocessing. The object detection AI model is replicated into several instances, and each instance processes a separate video segment in parallel. The models run simultaneously separate processors. The outputs from all model replicas are combined to generate a unified object detection output, which is then used to trigger alerts, track objects, or analyze traffic patterns.

The Concurrent Flow pattern is applied in this example to achieve real-time object detection on multiple video streams from surveillance cameras. By dividing the video streams into segments and processing them in parallel, the edge server can efficiently utilize its processing units, significantly reducing inference time and enabling responsive surveillance operations in a smart city environment.

4.3 Cascade Flow

Description
The Cascade Flow pattern in edge computing involves a sequential arrangement of multiple AI models, where the output of one model serves as the input to the next model in a cascading manner. This pattern is employed to achieve ordered processing, where each AI model specializes in a particular aspect of data analysis, leading to enhanced accuracy and efficiency in complex tasks.

Approach
The Cascade Flow pattern focuses on creating a pipeline of AI models that work together in a sequential manner. The output of each model is carefully processed and prepared to serve as input to the subsequent model, allowing for specialized analysis and decision-making at different stages of the pipeline.

Realization
The implementation of the Cascade Flow pattern includes some key aspects:

- Data collection: IoT devices or sensors collect raw data. This data can be in the form of sensor readings, images, audio, or video.
- Sequential AI Model Deployment: Multiple AI models are deployed sequentially in a cascading manner. Each model focuses on a specific analysis or task.
- Data Preprocessing and Transformation: The output of each model is preprocessed and transformed to match the input requirements of the subsequent model, including feature extraction, normalization, or formatting.
- AI Model Inference: The preprocessed data from the previous stage is fed into the next AI model in the sequence for further analysis and processing.
- Result Aggregation and Post-Processing: The final output of the last AI model in the cascade is generated by aggregating the results from the entire pipeline. Post-processing steps may involve filtering, decision-making, or visualization.

Example
In medical image diagnosis, the Cascade Flow pattern is used to analyze medical images progressively, starting from identifying basic features to diagnosing complex conditions. Medical images, such as X-rays or MRIs, are collected from medical devices and sent

to the edge server for analysis. The Object Detection stage detects and localizes objects of interest (e.g., organs, anomalies). The Feature Extraction stage extracts detailed features from the detected objects. The Disease Classification stage classifies the medical condition based on the extracted features. Each model analyzes the data at its individual stage, contributing to the overall diagnostic process. The final diagnosis is determined by aggregating information from all models and applying medical guidelines and thresholds.

The Cascade Flow pattern is suitable for tasks that require a multi-level analysis approach, where each stage of the cascade performs a specialized analysis contributing to the final outcome. This pattern showcases how edge computing can orchestrate a sequence of AI models to progressively process and analyze data, enabling accurate and context-aware decision-making in real-time applications.

5 Mixed Run

5.1 Input Fusion

Description
The Input Fusion pattern in edge computing involves combining data from multiple sensors to create a comprehensive and accurate representation of the environment or object being observed. This pattern leverages the strengths of different sensors to enhance the quality of information and make more informed decisions. Input fusion is particularly valuable in scenarios where individual sensors might provide limited or noisy data, but their combination leads to improved insights.

Approach
The Input Fusion pattern follows an approach where data from various sensors is collected, synchronized, and integrated. The fusion process involves merging data streams, aligning timestamps, and applying algorithms to extract meaningful insights. The goal is to provide a holistic view that is richer and more reliable than what each individual sensor could provide.

Realization
The implementation of the Input Fusion pattern includes the following key aspects:

- Data Collection: Data is collected from multiple sensors, which can include cameras, LIDAR, ultrasonic sensors, GPS, accelerometers, gyroscopes, and more.
- Data Synchronization: Data streams from different sensors are synchronized to ensure that measurements are processed chronologically.
- Sensor Calibration: Sensor calibration is performed to correct biases, errors, and inconsistencies in sensor measurements.
- Data Fusion Algorithms: Various data fusion algorithms are applied to integrate sensor data. These can include techniques like Kalman filtering, particle filtering, Bayesian inference, or neural networks.
- Information Extraction: The fused data provides a comprehensive view of the observed phenomenon, resulting in enhanced accuracy, reduced noise, and improved situational awareness.

Example
In autonomous vehicle navigation, the Input Fusion pattern is used to combine data from diverse sensors to accurately determine the vehicle's position and orientation. The autonomous vehicle is equipped with various sensors, and sensor data is synchronized using precise timestamps to ensure alignment between measurements. Sensor calibration corrects inaccuracies in sensor measurements due to factors like sensor biases or environmental conditions. Kalman filtering is applied to combine GPS and IMU (Inertial Measurement Unit) data for real-time vehicle positioning. LIDAR and camera data are used to detect obstacles and identify road features. Fused sensor data provides accurate vehicle localization, enabling the vehicle to navigate safely and make real-time decisions based on its surroundings.

The Input Fusion pattern is essential for enhancing the accuracy and reliability of data in edge computing scenarios. By combining data from multiple sensors, edge systems can gain a more holistic understanding of the environment, leading to improved decision-making and performance. This pattern demonstrates how input fusion can be instrumental in achieving more capable edge computing applications, such as in autonomous vehicles, robotics, and industrial automation.

5.2 Hierarchical Conduit

Description
The Hierarchical Conduit pattern involves organizing AI tasks and processes in a hierarchical structure, where higher-level tasks encapsulate and coordinate lower-level tasks. This pattern is used to manage complex AI workflows by breaking them down into manageable subtasks, allowing for modularity, scalability, and efficient resource allocation.

Approach
The Hierarchical Conduit pattern utilizes a top-down approach where AI tasks are organized in a hierarchy. Higher-level tasks orchestrate the execution of lower-level tasks, allowing for the division of labor and specialization. Each level of the hierarchy focuses on specific aspects of the problem, enabling better control, optimization, and coordination.

Realization
The implementation of the Hierarchical Conduit pattern includes some key aspects:

- Data Ingestion: The initial step involves the collection of raw data originating from IoT devices or sensors. This data is then seamlessly channeled into the edge server, leveraging established communication protocols such as MQTT, CoAP, or HTTP.
- Hierarchical Task Decomposition: The AI workflow is decomposed into a hierarchical structure with different levels of tasks. Higher-level tasks encapsulate lower-level tasks and manage their execution.
- Task Execution and Coordination: Higher-level tasks orchestrate the execution of lower-level tasks. Lower-level tasks process data, perform analytics, or execute AI models based on their specialized roles.

- Resource Allocation: Resources such as processing power and memory are allocated based on the hierarchical structure. Higher-level tasks may have broader resource access, while lower-level tasks are optimized for efficiency.
- Result Aggregation: Results from lower-level tasks are aggregated and provided as inputs to higher-level tasks. Aggregated results contribute to decision-making or further analysis.

Example

In disaster response scenarios, autonomous drones are deployed for surveillance, search, and rescue operations. The Hierarchical Conduit pattern is applied to manage complex drone operations involving data collection, obstacle avoidance, object detection, and path planning. Drone sensors collect data, including images and environmental parameters, which is transmitted to the edge server that determines the drone's mission, defining areas to cover and objectives to achieve. The drone captures images, performs object detection, and classifies detected objects. The drone uses real-time environmental sensing to avoid obstacles in its flight path. The mission planning task receives more computational resources as it requires complex optimization. Object detection and obstacle avoidance tasks are optimized for real-time execution. The detection results and obstacle avoidance decisions are aggregated and used by the mission planning task to make informed decisions about the drone's flight path.

The Hierarchical Conduit pattern allows for the effective management of complex drone operations in disaster response scenarios. By decomposing the tasks into hierarchical levels and specializing each level for specific tasks, the AI workflow becomes more organized, scalable, and manageable. This pattern exemplifies how edge computing can empower autonomous systems to make intelligent decisions and adapt to dynamic environments.

5.3   Ensemble Method

Description

The Ensemble Method pattern involves the integration of predictions or decisions from multiple AI models to achieve a more accurate, robust, and reliable outcome. This pattern leverages the diversity of individual models to address uncertainties, reduce biases, and enhance the overall quality of predictions or decisions.

Approach

The Ensemble Method pattern adopts an approach where multiple AI models trained on diverse datasets work collaboratively to make predictions or decisions. The aggregated output from these models provides a more comprehensive and trustworthy result compared to relying on a single model.

Realization

The implementation of the Ensemble Method pattern includes the following key aspects:

- Data Ingestion: Raw data is collected from sensors and ingested into the edge server using communication protocols like MQTT, CoAP, or HTTP.

- Ensemble Model Selection: Multiple AI models are selected, each with distinct characteristics, architectures, or training data. The models can include decision trees, neural networks, SVMs, etc.
- Model Inference: Each selected model makes independent predictions or decisions based on the input data.
- Aggregation of Outputs: The outputs from all models are aggregated using ensemble techniques such as majority voting, weighted averaging, stacking, or boosting.
- Result Generation: The final prediction or decision is generated based on the aggregated output, which represents a collective judgment from the ensemble of models.

Example

In financial transactions, the Ensemble Method pattern is used to detect fraudulent activities by aggregating predictions from multiple models. Transaction data, including account details and transaction attributes, is collected from POS systems, and is sent to the edge server for analysis. Multiple AI models are chosen, including decision trees, random forests, and neural networks, each trained on different subsets of historical transaction data. Each model evaluates transaction data and makes a prediction regarding whether the transaction is fraudulent or not. If most models predict fraud, the aggregated output is "fraudulent." Confidence scores from each model are combined to generate a weighted average score. Models are iteratively trained to correct misclassifications made by previous models. The final decision about the transaction's legitimacy is determined by analyzing the aggregated outputs and applying a predefined threshold.

The Ensemble Method pattern harnesses the collective ability of multiple AI models to enhance decision-making accuracy and reliability. This pattern showcases how edge computing can leverage diverse model capabilities to achieve more robust predictions or decisions, particularly in scenarios where uncertainties and biases need to be mitigated.

6 Applying Patterns

To effectively apply patterns, we compare the pros and cons of each pattern in Fig. 2.

In the Single Task category, the regular pattern, with its linear and unconditional execution, offers simplicity and predictability, making it suitable for tasks where stepwise analysis suffices. Conversely, the branched pattern excels in dynamic environments where adaptive decision-making is essential, albeit requiring well-defined conditions to guide branching. The circular pattern maintains vigilance through continuous monitoring and iterative adaptation, delivering real-time insights crucial for dynamically changing systems.

In the Multitask category, the serial pattern capitalizes on its sequential execution for ordered tasks, while the concurrent pattern optimizes resource efficiency for high-throughput scenarios. The cascade pattern achieves specialized analysis through ordered model integration, ideal for multi-level decision-making processes.

Pattern	Pros	Cons
Regular	• Simple and straightforward. • Linear execution.	• Limited flexibility. • May not suit complex tasks.
Branched	• Adaptability based on conditions. • Decision-making.	• Requires effective condition definitions. • May complicate workflow.
Circular	• Continuous monitoring and adaptation. • Real-time updates.	• May lead to resource-intensive processing. • More complexity
Serial	• Sequential analysis for ordered tasks. • Predictable flow.	• Limited parallelization. • Can be slower for complex workflows.
Concurrent	• Efficient resource utilization. • High throughput.	• Complexity in task coordination. • May require synchronization.
Cascade	• Specialized analysis at different stages. • Hierarchical.	• Cumulative error propagation. • May require complex input transformations.
Input Fusion	• Enhanced data quality and accuracy. • Reduced noise.	• Complexity in merging data streams. • Requires sensor calibration.
Hierarchical	• Modular organization of tasks. • Scalability.	• Complex hierarchy management. • Resource allocation challenges.
Ensemble	• Improved prediction accuracy. • Bias reduction.	• Requires diverse model selection. • May require additional computation.

Fig. 2. Comparison of Edge AI Patterns

In the Mixed Run category, the input fusion pattern tackles data quality enhancement by merging heterogeneous sensor data, though at the cost of calibration complexity. The hierarchical pattern fosters modular task organization, enhancing scalability and management in complex workflows. Lastly, the ensemble pattern harnesses diverse models to enhance prediction accuracy and mitigate biases, at the expense of model selection diversity.

7 Conclusion

In the realm of edge computing, the deployment of AI has led to the evolution of various AI patterns that tailor solutions to diverse application scenarios. This paper extensively explores a spectrum of edge AI patterns, namely regular, branched, circular, serial, concurrent, cascade, input fusion, hierarchical, and ensemble patterns. Through their distinct characteristics, each pattern serves as a valuable tool in addressing the complexities and challenges posed by real-time data processing, decision-making, and resource constraints at the edge.

The selection of an appropriate AI pattern in edge computing is a nuanced decision that hinges on the specific context, system requirements, and objectives of the application. The presented patterns collectively enrich the techniques available for designers, developers, and engineers navigating the intricate landscape of Edge AI. As the field continues to evolve, the understanding and strategic deployments of these patterns are poised to play a pivotal role in advancing the capabilities of Edge AI systems and fostering innovation across diverse domains.

References

1. Ding, A.Y., Peltonen, E., Meuser, T., et al.: Roadmap for edge AI: a Dagstuhl perspective. ACM SIGCOMM Comput. Commun. Rev. **52**(1), 28–33 (2022). https://doi.org/10.1145/352 3230.3523235

2. Tziouvaras, A., Foukalas, F.: Edge AI for Industry 4.0: an Internet of Things approach. In: Proceedings of the 24th Pan-Hellenic Conference on Informatics, November 2020, pp. 121–126 (2021). https://doi.org/10.1145/3437120.3437289

3. Wu, Y., Zhang, L., Gu, Z., Lu, H.,Wan, S.: Edge-AI-driven framework with efficient mobile network design for facial expression recognition. ACM Trans. Embed. Comput. Syst. **22**(3), 1–17 (2023). https://doi.org/10.1145/3587038. Article No. 57

4. Raith, P., Rausch, T., Prüller, P., Furutanpey, A., Dustdar, S.: An end-to-end framework for benchmarking edge-cloud cluster management techniques. In: IEEE International Conference on Cloud Engineering (IC2E), CA, USA, pp. 22–28 (2022). https://doi.org/10.1109/IC2E55 432.2022.00010

5. Le, K., Le-Minh, K., Thai, H.: BrainyEdge: an AI-enabled framework for IoT edge computing. Inf. Commun. Technol. Express **9**(2), 211–221 (2023). https://doi.org/10.1016/j.icte.2021. 12.007

6. Narayanan, D., et al.: Pipedream: generalized pipeline parallelism for DNN training. In: Proceedings of 27th ACM Symposium on Operating Systems Principles, SOSP, vol. 19, pp. 1–15. ACM, New York (2019). https://doi.org/10.1145/3341301.3359646

7. Gamma, E., Helm, R., Johnson, R., Vlissides, J.: Design Patterns: Elements of Reusable Object-Oriented Software. Pearson Deutschland GmbH, Munich (1995)

8. Hewitt, E.: Technology Strategy Patterns: Architecture as Strategy. O'Reilly Media, Sebastopol (2018)

9. Davis, C.: Cloud Native Patterns: Designing Change-Tolerant Software. Simon and Schuster, New York (2019)

10. Ibryam, B., Huß, R.: Kubernetes Patterns. O'Reilly Media, Sebastopol (2022)

Author Index

Printed in the United States
by Baker & Taylor Publisher Services